QUALIFIED
for YOUR
ANOINTING

BRIAN KINSEY

www.BrianKinsey.com

Dust Jacket Press
P.O. Box 721243
Oklahoma City, OK 73172
www.dustjacket.com

Ordering information for print editions:
Quantity sales. Special discounts are available on quantity purchases by corporations, associations, and others. For details, check out at www.BrianKinsey.com.

Individual sales. Dust Jacket Press publications are available through most bookstores. They can also be ordered directly from Dust Jacket: Tel: (800) 495-0192; Email: info@dustjacket.com; www.dustjacket.com

Dust Jacket logos are registered trademarks of Dust Jacket Press, Inc.

Cover & interior design: D.E. West - www.zaqdesigns.com & Dust Jacket Creative Services

Printed in the United States of America

www.BrianKinsey.com

CONTENTS

CHAPTER 1

The One Thing You Lack

Every Christian faces two personal challenges. The first is to live a godly life and the second is to serve effectively in Jesus' name. The key to victory in both challenges is the anointing of God upon your life.

God has a unique purpose for your life, and He wants you to find and fulfill it. There are mountains God wants you to climb, valleys He wants you to persevere through, and territories He wants you to conquer and claim in His name and for His glory. But you can't do all this on your own. To help you accomplish your purpose, God gives you His Holy Spirit to be with you and empower you to succeed. When you have God's presence and power in your life through the Holy Ghost, there is no power in the world that can stand against you. Nothing can prevent you from becoming everything God has called you to be and accomplishing everything He has planned for you to do.

If God has called you to it, you can be sure He will lead you through it. However, that is not the daily experience of far too many Christians. Life is difficult. We face personal challenges, health problems, and relational conflict. We are trapped in patterns of self-defeating behavior, sometimes for years. God wants us to live victorious lives and fulfill His purpose on earth, but most of us would have to admit that simply isn't happening. Why not? The reason is simple. Though there is no power on earth that can derail God's plan for your life, there is one person who can keep you from it. That person is you.

THE WAR WITHIN

The biggest obstacle to victory any Christian will face is *the war within*. This is the internal struggle to overcome deeply engrained habits, patterns of behavior, emotional responses, perspectives on life, and ways of communicating with others that hinder us from fulfilling God's purpose. The person you are right now has been shaped in large part by your unique personal experiences—some good, others not so good—and how you have responded to those circumstances from childhood to the present. Whether you are aware of it or not, you have developed your own manner that feels comfortable—or at least tolerable—and is uniquely you. Some of your manners or idiosyncrasies help you serve God and His kingdom while others keep you from that goal. For example, you may have experienced some trauma in your early life that led you to adopt self-destructive and self-defeating behaviors as a way to cope with the pain. Now those behaviors or patterns actually increase your pain and prevent you from pursuing God's purpose. Or your past or present circumstances may torment you with anxiety, depression, or despair. While the causes of your negative emotions may be beyond your control, you need to learn new ways of responding to those circumstances. Otherwise, you will remain trapped in that cycle of negative thoughts, emotions, and behaviors, unable to move into the future God desires for you.

While your personal challenges are unique to you, God's desire for all of us is the same. He wants us to win the war within, and He offers us the power to do so. You can't do this on your own, but with God's help you most certainly can. My purpose in writing this book is to show you how to receive God's anointing, to abide in His presence, and to operate in His power so that you will win this inner battle. And that victory can start right now, today.

THE WAR WITHOUT

Even as you are engaging the war within, God's plan for your life is unfolding. I don't know exactly what God has in store for you, but I do know this much: it will move you out of yourself and into the world. God's purpose for you will involve bringing hope and healing to others. God wants to transform you so that you can live a life marked by victory, holiness, and power. When you do, you will make a genuine difference in the lives of others and bring honor to the name of Jesus Christ.

For a few of us, that involves a calling to full-time ministry. For most, it simply means living in a way that impacts the lives of others. That might be at home, in your community, or in your workplace. That impact might be seen through things like hospitality, generosity, community outreach, or meeting people's physical needs. It will certainly mean that Jesus Christ shines through you in a way that attracts others to him. Your life *will* have an impact on others.

If that sounds exciting, let me assure you it is. But just as you can't win the war within on your own, you can't win the war *without* alone either. Just as your inner patterns of thought and behavior can keep you from realizing God's purpose, there are *external* forces that work against our efforts to bring hope and help to the world. You need the Holy Ghost and His power to win the war within. You need the Spirit for this outer struggle too. Rest assured, God has anointed you and He has made available the power to move into the world on His behalf. Without a doubt, you will have an impact on those around you, through the power of God.

The question then is, how does this happen? How do we gain access to the presence and power of God so we can finally be free from our inner doubts, sins, and destructive attitudes and be released into the world? We receive God's power when we are filled with the gift of the Holy Ghost speaking with other tongues, which is God's anointing.

GOD'S ANOINTING

Whatever your background, personality, and past experiences, God wants you to advance on both fronts. He wants you to win the war within and move into the war without, moving into the world with hope and healing. God shapes your character, your attitude and your perspective through the lens of His word, and by His voice in your life prepares you for ministry. If you gain nothing else from this book, please understand this: When God gives you a job to do, He *always* provides His presence and power to accomplish His purpose. The term for that blessing of presence and power for a specific purpose is *anointing*. That special presence and power of God is your anointing.

We don't have to look far in Scripture to see examples of God's anointing at work. We see them in both the Old and New Testaments. Even Jesus depended on God's anointing to do the work of calling people to repentance and faith in Him. He described His own anointing this way: "The Spirit of the Lord is on me, because he has anointed me to proclaim good news to the poor. He has sent me to proclaim freedom for the prisoners and recovery of sight for the blind, to set the oppressed free, to proclaim the year of the Lord's favor" (Luke 4:18–19).

Later, Luke described Jesus' anointing, saying that it was widely known " how God anointed Jesus of Nazareth with the Holy Spirit and power, and how he went around doing good and healing all who were under the power of the devil, because God was with him" (Acts 10:38).

God's Presence + God's Power = God's Anointing. Jesus depended on that special touch from God in His life and ministry, and we do too.

God's anointing is not reserved only for those in professional ministry. It isn't true that only a select group of Christians, a spiritual elite, receive God's anointing while others struggle along without it. Anointing is for everyone, including you. The apostle Paul made that clear to believers in the church at Corinth. He wrote, "Now it is God who makes both us and you stand firm in Christ. He anointed us, set his seal of ownership on us, and put his Spirit in our hearts as a deposit, guaranteeing what is to come" (2 Corinthians 1:21–22).

The apostle John also confirmed that God intends all believers to experience anointing. "As for you, the anointing you receive from him remains in you, and you do not need anyone to teach you. But as his anointing teaches you about all things and as that anointing is real, not counterfeit—just as it has taught you, remain in him" (1 John 2:27).

Anointing is for every believer. And it is not reserved only for public ministry. Your anointing also provides for personal healing and transformation. For example, the apostle James instructed his readers to anoint those who are sick with oil: "Is anyone among you sick? Let them call the elders of the church to pray over them and anoint them with oil in the name of the Lord. And the prayer offered in faith will make the sick person well; the Lord will raise them up. If they have sinned, they will be forgiven" (James 5:13–15). This physical anointing with oil represents the actual presence of God with the person who is sick. And where the Spirit is, there is always power to overcome.

CLAIM YOUR ANOINTING

Throughout Scripture, we are told of the necessity of—and power associated with—receiving God's anointing. Yet too often we remain defeated in our personal lives and ministry. We fail to overcome the personal obstacles we face and as a result, miss out on fulfilling God's purpose for our lives. That happens when we choose not to avail ourselves of the presence and power of God that is available to us. We may convince ourselves that we don't deserve it, that we are not good enough to receive it, or that we are not qualified for it. Sometimes we lack the patience or determination to take hold of it.

Whatever the reason, the results are predictable: we languish in emotional negativity, fail to overcome the patterns of behavior that hold us back, and lack the spiritual power to accomplish the work God wants us to do. We give in to discouragement, depression, and defeat, rather than moving forward in the power of Christ.

However, those who do embrace their anointing see very different results. They experience spiritual transformation. They see healing and miraculous intervention. They begin to experience victory in places where they had seen only defeat. Though there are still struggles, they have the confidence that comes from living in the presence of God and experiencing His power. When we have God's anointing, we know that He is with us every step of the way.

That is what I want for you, my friend. I want you to receive your anointing. I long for you to know the daily presence and power of God. I want to see you win the war within and be empowered to take the hope and peace of Jesus into the world. I firmly believe that God is calling His church—He is calling you—to experience this anointing. The purpose of this book is to help you prepare for, receive, and move forward with the anointing of God on your life. When you do, there is no power on earth that can stand in your way.

YOUR NEXT STEP

My hope is that this book will be a guide for you in releasing God's anointing into your life. Your first step is to prepare for it. Part I will guide you through the four steps you must take to prepare yourself to receive God's anointing. First, I will show you beyond any doubt that you are 100 percent qualified to receive this blessing. Then we will reveal the mindset of expectancy and the power of your perspective, which is critical for receiving anything from God. You will learn how to be patient and endure as you await God's action. And finally, I will guide you in moving forward under God's anointing once you have received it.

Part II is a handbook on the four main anointings you can expect to receive from God. It is vital that you understand how these anointings operate so you will be able to recognize them, receive them, and use them in your inner and outer battles. We will do this by studying the life of King David of ancient Israel, who was said to be a man after God's own heart. From a human perspective, David was an unlikely candidate to lead God's people. But with God's anointing on him, David was able to access God's wisdom and power to lead His people in righteousness and truth.

According to most scholars David received not just one anointing, but three, at various junctures of his life. However, in my study it was revealed to me that there was a fourth anointing in his life. The final four chapters of this book will reveal the four anointings David experienced which you can expect also. These are the Promise, Praise, Power and Personal anointings. I will explain each one, what they are used for, and when you can expect to receive them. I will also give guidance on how these anointings function in your life and the major pitfall that prevents so many people from experiencing them. When we are finished, you will be ready, waiting, and fully prepared to move with God when He calls you.

My friend, I want to help you experience your destiny under the anointing of God. My deepest desire is that you will experience God's presence and power so that you can experience all that He has for you. I want you to rise above the helplessness and despair of self-defeating thoughts and habits. I long for you to break that pattern of helplessness, to be strong and powerful, and to be filled with the Holy Ghost. So I pray that God will bind and break whatever is hindering you from receiving His anointing. I pray that God will redeem you from any and every curse that may be on your life. And I pray that you will come into your anointing and that your personal life and ministry will be empowered and transformed by the presence and power of God. I am eager to take this journey with you. Let's take the next step together.

PART I

Prepare for Your Anointing

CHAPTER 2

Claim the Inheritance

God releases His anointing to those who understand their authority is only in the Name of Jesus Christ. So, the first step to receiving God's anointing is to experience the fullness of Bible salvation through Jesus Christ by obeying Acts 2:38. The Lord Jesus is the qualifier. His authority is sovereign. His blood cleanses all things, and in His Name, we are qualified.

What would it be like to receive a phone call telling you that you had received a great inheritance from a total stranger? Would you believe it? That's exactly what did happen to seventy people in Lisbon, Portugal. Luis Carlos de Noronha Cabral da Camara, a Portuguese aristocrat, chose the people at random from the phone book. And when the childless bachelor died at the age of forty-two, the beneficiaries got the call. All of them were shocked, and a few suspected it was some sort of scam. But the bequest was real enough. It had been made in front of two witnesses at a registry office, thirteen years before.

Whether you know it or not, you have received an inheritance too. And it is far more valuable than a house or a bank account. In fact, it is life transforming. It became part of your birthright the moment you were born again of the water and of the Spirit. That inheritance is the anointing of God upon your life, His presence and power. It's not a scam, and there are no further requirements to meet. All you have to do is claim it in Jesus' Name. This is your first step in experiencing the anointing of God.

YOUR INHERITANCE IS
AVAILABLE NOW

God's anointing is your heritage as a Christian. The apostle Paul spoke about this inheritance in the book of Colossians. Notice he referred to it as a present reality:

> *For this reason, since the day we heard about you, we have not stopped praying for you. We continually ask God to fill you with the knowledge of his will through all the wisdom and understanding that the Spirit gives, so that you may live a life worthy of the Lord and please him in every way: bearing fruit in every good work, growing in the knowledge of God, being strengthened with all power according to his glorious might so that you may have great endurance and patience, and giving joyful thanks to the Father, who has quali-*

*fied you to share in the inheritance of his holy
people in the kingdom of light. For he has rescued
us from the dominion of darkness and brought us
into the kingdom of the Son he loves, in whom we
have redemption, the forgiveness of sins.*
(Colossians 1:9–14)

Your inheritance is "in the kingdom of light." Many people think of God's kingdom as something that will happen in the future. They equate it with the afterlife or going to heaven when they die, but the Gospels make it clear that God's kingdom is not only a future hope, but also a present reality.

When Jesus came preaching and teaching in the towns and villages near Galilee, His message was that everyone who heard should, "Repent, for the kingdom of heaven is at hand" (Matthew 3:2; 4:17). The meaning of that phrase, "at hand" is essentially, "right here, right now." In other words, you don't have to wait to experience God's kingdom. It is already here—all around you and even within you (Luke 17:21). While Satan's power may still have a grip on much of the world, God's power is breaking through every barrier and can work powerfully through us right now. That was true in Jesus' time, and it is true today. God's kingdom is not a dream, a vision, or a wish; it is a present reality with immediate benefits.

Those who are considered "holy people in the kingdom of light" are not those who are super-spiritual, but all those who have received the glorious gift of the Holy Ghost and been baptized in His wonderful and excellent Name, and thus have been set apart or made holy for His kingdom and His glory.

Paul indicated that this status—being set apart by God as one of His people—bestows on you a share in the inheritance. He further defined this inheritance, saying that God has ". . . delivered us from the power of darkness and hath translated us into the kingdom of his dear son" (Colossians 1:13). In other words, your inheritance means that you are no longer a slave to the powers of darkness in this world, whatever they may be named: shame, anxiety, depression, greed, vain ambition, lust, anger, oppression, or the like. God has declared you free, and you are free indeed—free to do kingdom work.

YOU ARE ALREADY QUALIFIED

An inheritance is a gift. Unlike wages or rewards, it cannot be earned. There is nothing you must do to qualify for it. You receive the inheritance simply because you are part of the family, either by birth or adoption. If you are not part of the family, there are no steps you can take to make yourself eligible for an inheritance. You became qualified the moment you were born.

The same is true of your inheritance in the kingdom of God. There is nothing you can do to qualify yourself to receive it. Going to church doesn't do it. Praying and reading your Bible doesn't do it. Going on a mission trip does not do it. Even working in the nursery doesn't do it. All of those things are good things, but none of them qualify you for an inheritance in the kingdom of God.

Your family cannot qualify you either. This is not an inheritance that your Mom and Dad can hand down to you, no matter how well off they may be or how much clout they have in the world. Family relationships are a precious thing, but they do not qualify you for a share in the kingdom of God. Like all inheritances, it is entirely unearned by merit. Yet it is owed by birth. We are qualified for our spiritual inheritance by our new birth into the Kingdom.

You see, God created each of us in His image and likeness, and He asked us to live in a way that reflects His glory. He wanted our lives to be filled with and wholly characterized by faith and trust in Him. He expected that we would be willing recipients of His love and that in return we would love Him and others around us. He desired that we not feel lost, abandoned, despairing, or alone, but that we are always confident in placing our hope in Him. He promised that He would always be with us and that if we would honor Him with our whole life we would live with Him forever.

Unfortunately, we could not uphold our end of the deal. Each of us in our own way has rebelled against God, rejected His rule over our lives, and put our hope in earthly things rather than in God our creator. Our sin created a separation from God. On God's side, He has never shown us anything but kindness, love, providence, and protection. But on our side, we turned away from Him, sinning against Him, and bringing judgement upon ourselves. We created a great canyon between ourselves and God, and we can't bridge it on our own.

Graciously, God chose to provide a way. He didn't leave us in our sin and hopelessness. God chose to take action. He made a way for us to receive forgiveness and be reunited with Him. He himself bridged the gap so that we could once again experience fellowship with God. He did that through Jesus Christ.

At His baptism, the Holy Ghost came upon Jesus in a powerful way. He was empowered to do the work of God, possessing an authority that was unmeasured and unprecedented. He walked among men and women and lived a perfectly sinless and loving life. Then He consented to be handed over to the Romans, to be beaten, scourged, spit upon, and worse. Ultimately, He allowed Himself to be crucified. He gave up His life on our behalf by being nailed to a cross—a perfect sacrifice for our sins. But there is more to the story. Jesus did more than save us from sin. He reunited us with God, making us members of His family:

- "Yet to all who did receive him, to those who believed in his name, he gave the right to become children of God" (John 1:12).

- "But when the set time had fully come, God sent his Son, born of a woman, born under the law, to redeem those under the law, that we might receive adoption to sonship" (Galatians 4:4–5).

- "He predestined us for adoption to sonship through Jesus Christ, in accordance with his pleasure and will" (Ephesians 1:5).

By virtue of Christ's sacrificial death and triumphant resurrection, we have been granted a new status as sons and daughters of God. We've been adopted! And as full members of God's family, we are qualified to receive an inheritance. You and I could not qualify ourselves for this gift. Nobody on earth could do it. But Jesus was commissioned by God to do exactly that. Jesus has made all who believe in Him sons and daughters of God. As a believer in Jesus, you are already qualified to receive this inheritance.

YOUR INHERITANCE RELEASES POTENTIAL

Do you remember the Portuguese man who left his entire estate to total strangers? That inheritance consisted of a twelve-room apartment, a house, a car, and about $32,000. And remember that it was to be divided among seventy people. While I am sure they were delighted with the gift, what would they do with it? They couldn't all live in the apartment or all drive the same car. The inheritance would have to be sold off and divided up. Not all gifts are as useful as they first appear.

You might well be asking a similar question about your spiritual inheritance. What good is it? What does it do for me? If it isn't money or possessions, what in the world can I do with it? In fact, this inheritance is more valuable than any of those things, once you realize its value and how it operates in your life. You can understand the value of God's inheritance by looking through two different frames—the *now* and the *not yet*.

The *not yet* is probably what many of us are most familiar with. When you die, or after Jesus's return, whichever comes first, you have heaven to look forward to. There will be no more sickness or pain. No more wars or conflict. No more sin or evil. We will be fully and completely redeemed, and we will dwell in the house of the Lord forever. If the inheritance only consisted of that much, it would already be worth more than we could possibly imagine. But there is more. Your inheritance also includes a *now* aspect. Right now you receive two gifts as a child of God.

PRESENCE

The first gift is God's presence in your life every day. You received that gift when you were enabled to speak with other tongues as the Spirit gave you utterance. Some people mistakenly believe that God's only purpose for being present in your life is to keep you in line. It's as if God is always watching and waiting for you to slip up so He can condemn you. There may be people in your life who do that kind of thing, but this is not God's way. God's presence in your life is like that of a faithful friend. God loves you without condition and is on your side in every way. God wants what's best for you, and He has your back. None of us likes to feel alone, even on a good day. We certainly don't want to be alone when we experience hardship. Your inheritance means that you are never alone. God is always with you. And if you pay attention, you may even see Him in the eyes of a caring, compassionate friend.

POWER

The second *now* aspect of your inheritance is God's *power* in your life. Here's how the apostle Paul described it:

> *I pray that the eyes of your heart may be enlightened in order that you may know the hope to which he has called you, the riches of his glorious inheritance in his holy people, and his incomparably great power for us who believe. That power*

is the same as the mighty strength he exerted when
he raised Christ from the dead and seated him at
his right hand in the heavenly realms, far above
all rule and authority, power and dominion, and
every name that is invoked, not only in the present
age but also in the one to come.
(Ephesians 1:18 –21)

According to Paul, it's not a question of *whether* we have God's power in our lives. Paul told the people of the church at Ephesus that he was praying they would realize what was *already* true. God's incomparably great power is already at work in us who believe. The same power that raised Christ from the dead is available to you today. And that power brings two incredible benefits.

First, it gives us victory in the war within (see chapter 1). Each of us battles against our own temptations and sins, which arise from our unique background, experiences, defense systems, and other tendencies. Satan wages war against us. In our own power we would be defeated. There is no way to overcome our arrogance, ambition, lust, laziness, timidity, lack of faith, anxiety, or depression on our own. But by the power of God, we can win these inner battles. We can put off the old self and put on the new. We can escape our slavery to sin and the devil and be free to serve Christ in joy and love. This is our inheritance.

Second, God's power also enables us to move into the world with Christ's message of love and peace. Through the Holy Spirit, He gives us everything we need to go up against principalities and powers, to share the message of God's love and transformation, to declare freedom from bondage, to speak words of healing and reconciliation, and to advance and support God's kingdom on earth. This too is our inheritance.

Remember the definition of God's anointing. It is God's presence and His power. This is our inheritance as children of God. As a believer in Jesus, you are fully qualified to receive that anointing right now. No one can disinherit you.

NO ONE CAN DISINHERIT YOU

Your inheritance is secured under Jesus' name. As long as you are in Christ, meaning part of His family through faith, that blessing is yours. No one can take it away. Pay close attention to the way the apostle Paul explains this:

> For those who are led by the Spirit of God are the children of God. The Spirit you received does not make you slaves, so that you live in fear again; rather, the Spirit you received brought about your adoption to sonship. And by him we cry, "Abba, Father." The Spirit himself testifies with our spirit that we are God's children. Now if we are children, then we are heirs—heirs of God and co-heirs with Christ, if indeed we share in his sufferings in order that we may also share in his glory. (Romans 8:14–17)

The only way you could be disinherited is if God failed you by not keeping His promises —and you know that's not going to happen. As long as you remain in Christ, no one can take that away from you.

That is not to say that some people won't try. There are always a few people who are more interested in tearing down others than in doing anything productive with their own life. At some point, they may take aim at you. They might question what right you have to claim an anointing. They might even question the very concept of anointing. That can be difficult to bear, especially coming from people who are close to you. Just remember you have been qualified by Jesus to receive your anointing. You are part of his family. You are an heir. No one can take that away from you. Stand firm and rest assured, knowing that you are in Christ. Remember what Paul said, "The Spirit himself testifies with our spirit that we are God's children" (Romans 8:16). Trust the Spirit.

Sometimes though, we sabotage ourselves. We do this when we tell ourselves that we don't deserve the anointing. Or we begin to think the anointing is only for those who are somehow better than we are. Or we become timid, fearing what will happen in our lives if we claim God's anointing. When that happens, exchange that negative inner voice with the powerful Word of God. Pray the Word of God over yourself. Speak the truth into your own heart, reminding yourself that God has claimed you, adopted you into His family, and given you a purpose. Remind yourself that when God gives you something to do, He always provides the power to do it.

Many people worry that they have somehow disqualified themselves from the anointing. They might say, "You don't know the things I've done or all the ways I've sinned against God. Maybe I was qualified at one time, but I just don't feel it anymore." Weighed down by sin and shame, they fear that God is done with them. They come to believe that while they once qualified for God's anointing, they don't anymore.

There is no question that sin is a serious thing. It hurts people, breaks relationships, and offends a holy God. Yet there is only one sinless person, Jesus. So if sinlessness was what qualified us for anointing, only one would ever have been anointed. We are qualified for God's anointing not by being sinless, but by the precious blood of Jesus Christ, the only sinless one. He qualifies us by His sacrifice. Being sinless doesn't qualify you for God's anointing. It is God's anointing that enables you to be holy in His sight. Trying to earn your anointing only makes you proud of yourself and resentful of others. Simply receive the gift by faith.

CLAIM YOUR ANOINTING
IN JESUS' NAME

The news only gets better from here. You don't have to wait to receive your inheritance. It is not something we look toward in the distance or can expect only when we get to heaven. As a believer in Jesus, you are already qualified to receive this inheritance. Because He died and rose again, any who are saved are adopted into God's family. That work is already done. So all you have to do is claim your inheritance and take hold of it:

Jesus made that very clear when he said,

Very truly I tell you, whoever believes in me will do the works I have been doing, and they will do even greater things than these, because I am going to the Father. And I will do whatever you ask in my name, so that the Father may be glorified in the Son. You may ask me for anything in my name, and I will do it.

Very truly I tell you, my Father will give you whatever you ask in my name. Until now you have not asked for anything in my name. Ask and you will receive, and your joy will be complete. (John 14:12–14; 16:23–24)

Jesus wanted his disciples to have victory over sin and over the powers of darkness that would prevent them from being and doing everything God had called them to. He told them to pray *in His name.*

The words "in Jesus' name" are often appended to prayers in a perfunctory, even mindless way. We may add them because other people do or because that's what we have been taught. Such use of Jesus' name is pointless, even sacrilegious. To be sure, there is power in the name of Jesus. When we pray intentionally and meaningfully in the name of Jesus, we release that power. Jesus is God. He is both Lord and Christ, and He is the King of Kings. He is sovereign over all creation. He secured our salvation and redemption. And he has the power to break sin's curse and its hold over us. He has the power to transform our lives. When we pray in the name of Jesus we acknowledge that He is the giver of life. It is through Him that we have been qualified for our anointing. So when we pray in His name, we pray in His power and by His authority.

If you want to live in your anointing, there is nothing more important for you to do than to trust in the name of Jesus. Make His name large in your life. Say His name. Make mention of Him frequently. Speak well of Him, just as you would a trusted friend. Lift up His name. Exalt Him. Praise the matchless name of Jesus.

To make Jesus large in your life, make Him first in your heart. Get to know Him better every day by meditating on His word. Remember the many ways He has already shown that He loves you. Make communing with Jesus a priority in your daily life. Learn to trust Him as someone who always wants what is best for you.

And keep it real. Jesus is not a fantasy hero. He is both God and a flesh-and-blood human being. He is a person that could be touched, bumped into, hugged, beaten, and crucified. He lived on earth to show us what it means to be human, to demonstrate what can happen when we are anointed by God, and to qualify us for our inheritance.

The prophet Isaiah urged us to, "Seek the Lord while he may be found; call on him while he is near" (Isaiah 55:6). And the apostle Paul promised, "Everyone who calls upon the name of the Lord will be saved" (Romans 10:13). Today is the day to call on the name of Jesus and find victory in your life.

You have an inheritance. It is yours by virtue of whose you are. You are qualified, because Jesus paid the price for your sins; God adopted you into His family, and the Holy Spirit filled your life with His presence. There's nothing more for you to do other than claim the anointing as your own. When you do, you will take a gigantic step toward becoming everything God created you to be and to do. You will have the power you need in your life to defeat the sin that so easily entangles you. And you will have the power to make a difference in your neighborhood, your community, and your world, for Jesus. If you are ready to claim your inheritance—to receive your anointing—continue with me on this journey as we examine the need for patience, endurance, and joy.

ANOINTING IN ACTION

If you haven't already, lay claim to your inheritance today. God wants you to experience His freedom in every area of your life and to do the work He has given you. But you have to take that first step of claiming your inheritance, of receiving your anointing. Here's what you can do today.

First, profess your faith in Jesus, ask His pardon for your sin, be baptized in the name of the Lord Jesus Christ, receive the wonderful gift of the Holy Ghost, and take your place in God's family. You can do that with a heart of faith and obedience.

Second, accept the truth that no one can disqualify you from the inheritance Jesus has provided. It is your right, by faith. If you have any unconfessed sin, confess it now to ensure that you have a clear relationship with Jesus.

Third, ask Jesus to release His power into your life. Make Jesus large in your life by making Him your first priority and communing with Him daily. Be expectant and ready.

Finally, be vigilant for the Spirit's leading. You will begin to identify places in your life where you need to grow. And you will begin to understand the work God has prepared for you to do. When you hear the Spirit's voice, say yes every time.

CHAPTER 3

Patiently Prepare

Your anointing is fixed, but the timing is flexible. God will release it when He is ready and when you are ready. In the meantime, patiently prepare yourself to receive the gift.

A friend of mine preached the funeral of a very precious saint in Houston, Texas. Her name would be unknown to most who would read this book; however, her story was remarkable because of her tremendous patience and uncommon courage.

She had a terrible affliction of arthritis and was continually in pain, but because she had a family to feed and children to care for, she would rise at four o'clock in the morning and walk to catch a bus that would take her to work. She would work all day and then catch the bus and ride back home. In the wintertime it would be dark when she left home and dark again before she returned. Yet she was faithful. What patience! What courage!

Her patience and faithfulness are almost unheard of today. This precious, frail lady never missed church and was loyal to her family and her God to the very end. My preacher friend called it "four o'clock in the morning courage," describing her faithfulness in the face of such adversity and her testimony of excellence.

It is no wonder he felt compelled to honor her with such a superb title. In a world where few of us want to wait more than two minutes for a food order, patient endurance is an extremely rare quality. Yet that is exactly what we need in order to fully experience the anointing of God.

As one who belongs to Jesus, you are qualified to receive the power of the Holy Ghost to gain victory in every area of life. Yet that doesn't mean that you will experience immediate, automatic success in all your endeavors. God's Spirit is beyond our control. We often wish for God to do more than what He is doing, or to do it more quickly. But we cannot dictate the Spirit's timetable. Only God can determine when His power will be released in our lives. In His infinite wisdom, He does what is in all of our best interests. Having claimed our share in God's anointing, our next task is to wait patiently and expectantly for God to move. Let's look again at an excerpt from Paul's letter to the Colossians:

> *For this reason, since the day we heard about*
> *you, we have not stopped praying . . that you may*
> *live a life worthy of the Lord and please him in ev-*
> *ery way: bearing fruit in every good work, growing*

in the knowledge of God, being strengthened with
all power according to his glorious might so that
you may have great endurance and patience, and
giving joyful thanks to the Father, who has quali-
fied you to share in the inheritance of his holy
people in the kingdom of light.
(Colossians 1:9–12)

This passage describes key qualities that often precede, or at least coincide with, the anointing that releases God's power in our life. Let's examine each of them more closely. As you begin to exhibit these qualities, you will gain confidence that you are perfectly positioned for God to release His power through you.

ENDURANCE

Paul wrote that he wanted his readers to have great endurance. In one sense, endurance is almost a given for all of us. No matter what happens, we endure it. Think of it this way, you have already endured every challenge you have ever faced. When trials come, it is sink or swim. Either we endure or we die. So far, we've endured!

For my part though, if I have to swim I want to do more than tread water. I would like to put a little *swag* in my stroke and come out of the pool with a smile on my face. For a Christian, endurance means more than simply surviving. It includes a refusal to be defeated by the evil one. This is not motivated by pride but by a sincere trust in Jesus and the desire to live in a manner worthy of His investment in us. Endurance means saying, "I'm going to do the right thing, even if I get what seems like a bad outcome." It is a determination to engage the world in a way that brings glory to God, no matter what.

Scripture is full of examples of godly endurance. Think of Abraham waiting decades for a son and an heir before having Isaac at age one hundred. Or think of Jacob being virtually exiled from his family, then working fourteen years to marry the woman of his dreams. Jacob's son Joseph had to bear the indignity of being sold into slavery by his own brothers and being unjustly imprisoned by the pharaoh before being vindicated and placed in a position of leadership. Study the Scriptures and you will see that endurance is a common trait among God's people. From Moses to Joshua to Samuel to David, not to mention the apostles, God's people have endured opposition, persecution, and even martyrdom in carrying out their calling.

Our greatest example of endurance is Jesus, as the author of Hebrews says: "Let us run with perseverance the race marked out for us, fixing our eyes on Jesus, the pioneer and perfecter of faith. For the joy set before him he endured the cross, scorning its shame, and sat down at the right hand of the throne of God. Consider him who endured such opposition from sinners, so that you will not grow weary and lose heart" (Hebrews 12:2 –3). Jesus knew exactly what He was going to face. That's why He experienced such agony in the Garden of Gethsemane on the evening of His arrest. More than any of us, He understood that carrying out God's will on earth requires the ability to endure. And Jesus was able to do so because of "the joy set before him."

As we remember the example of Jesus, we will let go of any attitudes that may be dragging us down. We will give up on the idea that receiving the power of God will happen easily, quickly, and without some cost on our part. We will be enabled to endure. Put aside any ways of thinking that may be limiting what God can do in your life. Power through any challenges you are facing to continue on the path God has laid out for you. Endure because you know that God will do all that He has promised, in His time and in His way.

PATIENCE

If endurance has to do with our *actions*—carrying on in the face of adversity—patience has to do with the *attitude* we have as we endure. There is a kind of endurance that could hardly be called patient. Maybe you've seen it before, or just maybe you have been there yourself. It's when we know that we have to keep going but decide we don't have to be happy about it. We grumble, whine, and complain—if not to others, at least to ourselves. We think negative thoughts. We fail to see the good things. We let our circumstances drag us down, so that our attitude becomes a liability rather than an asset. We may endure, but certainly don't do so with joy and patience.

There is nothing wrong with expressing your feelings when circumstances get you down. In fact, it is good and important for you to do that, and much better than stuffing those feelings down inside of you and pretending they don't exist. If you do that, they will eventually explode into a fit of anger or resentment. But there is a difference between venting your feelings and wallowing in them. If you are struggling with your emotions, find a trusted friend and let it all out. And let that be the end of it. Pivot to hope, believing that God is faithful. Hope is the foundation of patience.

Patience is that inner calm and assurance that enables you to believe that God will move, even if that takes longer than you would like. Patience requires trusting God's timing and His faithfulness. You might have difficulty understanding why God waits to bless you and your church in ways that are undeniable and even miraculous. But patience says, "I refuse to rush God. I'm seeking His blessing earnestly, but I don't want to receive the outpouring of power even one minute before I am ready to steward it appropriately and maximize its impact." Patience believes that God will act when it is time to act, so we don't need to concern ourselves about it.

Job is the classic example of patience. As you may know, Job had it all—wealth, power, family—all the external signs that seem to point to God's blessing on one's life. Then, he lost it all in a moment, not due to any failing on his own part but because God allowed it. Job had a lot of feelings about what had happened to him, but he did not let those feelings rule his life. He clearly and unapologetically shared his thoughts and emotions with the friends who had come to sit with him in the presence of God. Job did not hold back, but neither did he let those feelings get the best of him. While being completely honest and transparent about what was going on inside him, he maintained his faith in God and made clear to his friends that God was his hope.

Few of us have experienced the level of suffering that Job experienced so our frustrations can hardly compare. But we learn from Job's example what it means to have patience and trust that God has our best interests at heart, even when it's hard for us to understand what he Has in mind.

JOYFUL THANKS

Paul mentioned another quality that often precedes the outpouring of God's anointing when he wrote that we are to be "giving joyful thanks to the Father." If we are honest, most of us have a little trouble with that. That phrase "joyful thanks" packs a powerful punch. First, it calls for gratitude. That involves recognizing that everything we have is a gift from God. He does not owe us anything. We don't deserve anything from Him. We cannot earn anything or put God in our debt in any way. God is responsible for every good thing in our life—every material possession, every relationship, every opportunity, every achievement, every little bit of success we experience. Gratitude recognizes God's graciousness and responds with thankfulness. And when your heart is filled with true thankfulness, there's little room left for any sadness or disappointment over anything you don't have yet.

The second thing that little phrase calls for is joy. Joy is different than pleasure. It is deeper than happiness. It is one of the most positive, life-affirming, satisfying experiences a person can have. Joy comes from knowing that God genuinely loves us, treasures us, and has deep, lasting affection for us. It flows out of the truth that God is on our side, that He wants what is best for us, and is determined to bring about our ongoing transformation, continually equipping us for everything He is calling us to do. Joy involves knowing that God's plan will be completed in our life and in the world.

The apostle Paul knew something about joy in the midst of adversity. He was whipped, shipwrecked, beaten and left for dead, and falsely imprisoned. Yet he was determined not to let his difficult circumstances rob him of his joy in Christ. Even in prison, Paul's attitude never sagged. He wrote to the Philippians:

> *Now I want you to know, brothers and sisters, that what has happened to me has actually served to advance the gospel. As a result, it has become clear throughout the whole palace guard and to everyone else that I am in chains for Christ. And because of my chains, most of the brothers and sisters have become confident in the Lord and dare all the more to proclaim the gospel without fear. . . .*
>
> *The important thing is that in every way, whether from false motives or true, Christ is preached. And because of this I rejoice.*
>
> *Yes, and I will continue to rejoice, for I know that through your prayers and God's provision of the Spirit of Jesus Christ what has happened to me will turn out for my deliverance. . . . For to me, to live is Christ and to die is gain.*
> (Phil. 1:12—21)

Later in the same letter, Paul said that we should have the same attitude: "Rejoice in the Lord always. I will say it again: Rejoice!" (Phil. 4:4).

You cannot endure with a sour spirit. You cannot be patient with a bad attitude. If you are going to endure and be patient, you've got to do it joyfully. And if we do it joyfully, we can give thanks to the Father "who has qualified you to share in the inheritance of his holy people in the kingdom of light" (Col. 1:12). It is hard to wait. There's no question about it. But know that God's not through with you yet. He is just getting started. Your trial is making you competent. Your "disaster" is increasing your capacity to receive more of what God has promised you—if you wait with joyful thanks.

STRENGTH

All of this may sound rather daunting. You may wonder whether you can do it or how you will measure up. It is important to realize that God does not expect us to endure, be patient, and give joyful thanks in our own power. We are not left on our own to figure out a way over, under, around, or through the obstacles in our path. That is why the apostle Paul said that while we are seeking to walk worthy of our Lord and step into our anointing, we are "being strengthened with all power according to his glorious might" (Col. 1:11).

Notice that Paul did not say we are strengthening ourselves. He didn't say that God is waiting for us to go to the gym to work out and bulk up a bit. Instead, Paul used the passive form of the verb. We are "being strengthened." The strengthening is not something we do ourselves but something that is done to us. As we seek Him, God imparts His "glorious might." When it comes to adding strength, it doesn't get any better than that. No one is stronger or more powerful than the God of the universe—and He wants to infuse us with His strength to accomplish His purposes.

And that's not all. Consider those two little words: "all power." Paul did not say that God is strengthening us with a little power or with some of His power. God is strengthening us with *all* power. When God gives us a job to do, He always gives us His power to do it. When we are strengthened by God, we don't have to worry about whether we will have what it takes to get the job done. We can believe and trust that God's power and might will be sufficient for all of our needs.

However, being strengthened does not come automatically, nor does it necessarily come at the time of our choosing. God's Spirit acts in His own time and way. That is why there is a need for patience and endurance as we seek to live out our anointing. Sometimes, the reason that we are not seeing the results we desire is that we are not yet strong enough to handle what would happen if God acted through us in the way that we desire. How much better to wait on God's timing than to try to force His hand and launch out in our own failing strength. As we gain God's strength, we are better able to handle the anointing that is to come.

KNOWLEDGE

The apostle Paul assured us that while we are seeking to step into our anointing, it is always worthwhile to "grow in the knowledge of God" (Col. 1:10). Those of us who have been followers of Christ for quite some time may think that we already know God, so there is not much more that we need to learn. What a mistake! The God we serve is inexhaustible. None of us could learn everything there is to know about God, even if we spent eternity studying Him. Those of us who thought we knew God when we were young have learned through the experience of years that there are depths to Him that we could never have fathomed when we were just starting out. We don't acquire true knowledge of God from a few years of study—far from it. Knowing God is the pursuit of a lifetime.

Come to God with a humble heart, seeking to know Him and His ways more and more each day. And keep in mind that there are at least two types of knowledge of God. First is what we might call book knowledge, even though it can be acquired in other ways than through books. This is the kind of knowledge that comes from the study of or discussion on the Bible, Apostolic doctrine, and theology. This kind of learning yields facts about God, beliefs, perspectives, theories, and opinions. This is the kind of knowledge that can be distilled into words and written down in books or posted on the internet. This knowledge is valuable and even essential. If you don't know anything *about* God, then how can you know God?

However, there is a second type of knowledge that is rarer but just as important. This is what we might call experiential knowledge of God. This knowledge comes through a genuine relationship with a person. Think of the difference this way. Book knowledge is like reading a person's social media profiles to learn facts about them. These days, it's possible to learn a lot about a person you have never actually met. Experiential knowledge is different. It is based in real, in-person interactions. It comes from listening, observing, asking questions, sharing life and experiences and feelings. A person who has only book knowledge of God might be able to teach a class about theology, even a very insightful class. But it takes experiential knowledge to lead—or even participate in—a move of God. As someone who is pursuing God's anointing, it is essential that you grow in genuine knowledge of God through personal relationship with Him.

FRUIT BEARING

Paul mentioned one more prerequisite for anointing that is often overlooked: "bearing fruit in every good work" (Col 1:10). Typically, we think of "fruit" as our overall impact on others—people won to truth through our ministry; people who found emotional, spiritual, or physical healing; people who discovered their calling or received their anointing as a direct result of our ministry with them. However, the apostle Paul more often talked about fruit as evidence of God's transformation in a person's life. Consider the "fruit of the spirit" Paul listed in another letter:

> But the fruit of the Spirit is love, joy, peace, longsuffering, gentleness, goodness, faith, Meekness, temperance: against such there is no law. And they that are Christ's have crucified the flesh with the affections and lusts. If we live in the Spirit, let us also walk in the Spirit. Let us not be desirous of vain glory, provoking one another, envying one another. (Galatians 5:22–26)

Knowledge is deceitful. Just because a person knows about God doesn't necessarily mean that they *know* God and are being transformed by Him. One thing that doesn't lie is a person's behavior. Paul says that you can tell whether a person is living by the flesh or the Spirit by the fruits of their life.

Many people seek anointing, impact, and even great renown in ministry. But how many seek the fruit of the Spirit—love, joy, peace, forbearance, kindness, goodness, faithfulness, gentleness, and self-control? While seeking to step into your anointing, don't neglect to grow in these life-transforming attitudes and behaviors. They are what truly reflect one's connection with Christ and His work in one's life. Bearing fruit is one of the best evidences that you are ready to receive God's promised anointing.

ANOINTING IN ACTION

It's all too easy to focus on what God is *not* doing in our lives. We often expect God to do great things in our time and our way rather than trusting His perfect will and timing. Rather than obsess over our lack of apparent ministry results or complain that God is not using us in the way that we would like, Paul gave us these simple, practical ways to focus our attention on what really matters—and on what will prepare us for His anointing. Be intentional about developing these qualities in your life. As you do, God will strengthen and prepare you to receive the great gift of His anointing. Here are some specific ways you can prepare yourself for God's work in you.

First, find one of the biblical examples of endurance mentioned in the chapter and spend some time thinking about it.

What do you think made their situation difficult to endure? What helped them to endure? What can you learn about endurance that might apply to your life?

Second, make a list of activities in your life that can help you maintain calm and be patient. These might include reading the Bible, praying, meditating, taking a walk, spending time with a trusted friend, or any number of other activities. Choose one of the activities from your list to do the next time you feel impatient with God's timing.

Finally, identify which of the two ways described in this chapter that you have typically relied on to grow in the knowledge of God—book knowledge or experiential knowledge. Then seek to grow in the other. If you are most comfortable with book knowledge, seek experiential knowledge, and vice versa.

CHAPTER 4

Hold Out Hope

Neither anticipating nor living in God's anointing is always easy. It is possible to become disheartened by the waiting or the perceived lack of results in our work. We need hope to remain passionate, expectant, and encouraged.

November 2, 2016, is a date that will go down in history. On that day, the Chicago Cubs beat the Cleveland Indians to win the World Series and become baseball's reigning champions for the first time in 108 years. The previous time the Cubs won the Series, Theodore Roosevelt was president of the 46 United States of America, Mark Twain was still alive, radio and the airplane were both newfangled inventions, and the periodic table contained 85 rather than 118 elements. The Cubs had endured the longest drought in baseball history, and it challenged the patience of even their most ardent fans.

Every spring, Cubs fans seemed to repeat the same mantra: "This could be the year." And every year for over a century, they saw that hope dashed. "Oh well," they concluded, "There's always next year." Their team had become known as the loveable losers of the National League. And the fans, it seemed, had gone beyond devoted to delusional. After the climactic seventh game of the 2016 series, which went to extra innings after a rain delay, further heightening the anticipation, the depth of the fans' dedication became evident. Younger fans celebrated with shouts of joy, but many older fans broke into quiet tears. News images showed nursing home residents in their eighties and nineties, blissfully smiling at the news of victory. Hazel Wilson, who was born in Chicago in August of 1908, shortly before the Cubs' previous win, was believed to be the only Cubs fan to have been alive for both victories. As she watched from her home in New Hampshire, she said, "It was worth every inning." Other than Hazel, every Cubs fan on earth had waited their entire lifetime to see their team rise to victory. At last, that longsuffering devotion was rewarded. Their hope was rewarded by victory.

Many sports fans understand the concept of hope, which, if we are honest, is difficult for many Christians to grasp. We understand faith, which is trust in an unseen God. And we see the beauty of love, which is unconditional commitment to another. But hope is harder to grasp. Yet there it is, listed by the apostle Paul as one of the three crowning virtues of the Christian life: "And now these three remain: faith, hope, and love" (1 Corinthians 13:13). So what is Christian hope? And how does it impact our desire for God's anointing?

Our anointing is promised, as we have already seen. And we are qualified for it by faith in Christ. But it doesn't necessarily come to fruition at the time or in the manner that we expect. Most of us experience a period of waiting. While we can spend that time profitably by developing the qualities that make us able to receive and use our anointing wisely, the waiting can be difficult. During that time, it is hope that keeps us going. Hope is a deep-seated belief that, no matter what frustrations we may be experiencing right now, the best is yet to come. Hope touches all aspects of our being: mind, heart, and will. When we are full of hope in Christ, there is nothing that can distract us or keep us from enduring in the power of Christ and living into our full anointing. You can maintain that faithful endurance for as long as needed when you understand the three essential aspects of hope.

THE NATURE OF HOPE

The nature of hope is that it is future focused. It is a virtue we experience now, but it is entirely focused on the strong belief and firm assurance that the best is yet to come through Christ. Let's look closer at the future orientation of hope to see how it impacts our ability to live in the present.

VISION

Genuine Christian hope always involves our minds. It is never irrational, even if it defies worldly logic. It requires learning to think about our present circumstances and future possibilities as God might see them. It means having the mind of Christ. Hope depends on having a vision for the future. Hope is not, as some people suppose, a state of denial about the present. We can see the brutal reality in which we are currently living. Just like Jesus in the Garden of Gethsemane, we must come face-to-face with the difficult road we have been called to walk. Yet we also see what lies at the end of the journey. In Jesus' situation, the author of Hebrews describes that as "the joy set before him." Jesus knew that if He completed His work on earth, including giving His life on the cross, He would be raised again as the firstfruits of all those who will one day experience resurrection. He could envision that His death would result not only in His own resurrection, but also in the resurrection of many "brothers and sisters" who believe in Him. That includes you and me. Because Jesus could picture that outcome in His mind's eye, He was able to endure the worst that humanity could throw at Him.

Vision is the fuel for hope. When you begin to envision the things that will surely happen when you finally step into your full anointing—the lives that will be changed, the relationships that will be restored, the communities that will experience transformation, the individuals who will experience their own anointing in Christ—you will be inspired to keep the faith. Hope engages our minds with vision.

EXPECTATION

Genuine Christian hope also touches the heart. Hope is not merely something we believe but something we feel at the core of our being. As we do, we move beyond having a vision of what is possible to having an expectation of what God will indeed make happen. If we know God's promises but don't expect them to come to pass, we do not have genuine hope.

Going back to the example of Jesus in the garden, we see that Jesus not only had an intellectual understanding of God's promises about what would happen when he endured the cross and the grave, but it stirred His heart so that He felt joyful expectation. Hope moves us emotionally so that we live in expectation that the best is yet to come.

ANTICIPATION

The future orientation of hope affects our will also. It changes our behavior by influencing the choices we make on a daily basis. Our actions display anticipation for what is to come. Jesus illustrated that point in a story recorded in Matthew 25. In the parable, ten virgins went out to wait for the arrival of the bridegroom. Five of them were foolish and five were wise. The foolish ones took their lamps but did not take any oil with them. The wise ones, however, took oil in jars along with their lamps. The bridegroom was a long time in coming. When the time came to meet him, the foolish ones realized they did not have enough oil to keep their lamps lit. They had to return to town and buy more. As a result, they missed the wedding banquet while the five wise virgins were able to enter. The wise virgins demonstrated genuine hope. They believed and expected that the bridegroom was coming. They anticipated that arrival by choosing to bring the extra oil.

In the same way, when we really expect God's help, we will live as though it could come at any moment. Our choices will be based on that anticipation. That is the essence of hope: believing, feeling, and acting as if God will do just what He said He would do, in His own time and His own way.

THE OBJECT OF HOPE

Let's return for a moment to the subject of sports. The Cubs fans mentioned earlier seemed to display genuine hope. They lived in constant expectation that "this could be the year." The Cubs' victory in 2016 seems to validate the fans' hope. But does it? Was there really a guarantee that the Cubs would win another World Series? Was there some authority who had promised that their day would come? No, there was not. Those fans simply chose to believe in an outcome that they passionately wanted, not one that was guaranteed. And that is the difference between what many people think of as hope and the Christian concept of hope. Our hope is not in our own dreams and desires. It has a much firmer object than that. We hope in the person, promises, and inheritance of Jesus Christ.

THE PERSON OF CHRIST

First and foremost, we place our hope in a person. Our hope is in Christ himself. If Christians have any right or reason to hope for anything, it is only because Jesus Christ lived, died, and was raised to new life. Jesus became one of us so that He could fully experience what it means to be human, to love and forgive, to be mistreated and persecuted, and to lay down one's life for others. Through His life, Jesus showed us what it means to live fully devoted to God. By His death, He made the way for us to receive forgiveness of sins and redemption. And through His resurrection, He gave us power to experience new life in him. It is Jesus who has qualified us for our anointing.

When we experience doubt, we can look to Jesus who has blazed the trail for us. Jesus not only paid the penalty for our sin; He also broke its power over us. That means we can have victory over every force that seeks to oppress our lives, whether from without or within. Jesus is our perfect example of putting doubt aside to pursue God's plan for our lives. Like Jesus, we can focus our sights on the joy that is set before us.

Our hope is not in an earthly or religious system, or in ourselves, and it is certainly not in our own aspirations. Our hope is in Jesus, the author and finisher of our faith, and He will never let us down. Our hope in Christ will never disappoint us.

THE PROMISES OF CHRIST

Because Christ is totally trustworthy, we can also place our hope in His promises to us. Everything He has promised will come true. You can absolutely count on it.

Christ's promises to us are many, and they mostly revolve around our redemption and restoration to God's original design for our lives. He promises that our lives do have meaning and significance to God. He promises that His sacrifice is sufficient to secure our eternal salvation. He promises that, as we submit our lives to Him, He will transform us into His image. He will never leave us, and we will never be alone. His love will surround us so that we are never unloved. He will produce the fruit of the Spirit in our lives.

Christ's promises are not for our lives only, but also for our ministries. He promises that when we preach the Word, it will not return void but will always produce a harvest. He promises that we will be empowered by the Holy Ghost to do His work in His name. We will never have to fight the Lord's battles in our own strength.

THE INHERITANCE OF CHRIST

Ultimately, we place our hope in the fact that we are children of God—brothers and sisters of Jesus, and share in His inheritance. Listen to the apostle Paul:

> *For those who are led by the Spirit of God are the children of God. The Spirit you received does not make you slaves, so that you live in fear again; rather, the Spirit you received brought about your adoption to sonship. And by him we cry, "Abba, Father." The Spirit himself testifies with our spirit that we are God's children. Now if we are children, then we are heirs—heirs of God and co-heirs with Christ, if indeed we share in his sufferings in order that we may also share in his glory.* (Romans 8:14-17)

Because we belong to Jesus, we are the children of God and joint heirs with Jesus. Ultimately, everything that belongs to Christ will belong to us too. That's why in his letter to the Ephesians, Paul said this:

> *In him we were also chosen, having been predestined according to the plan of him who works out everything in conformity with the purpose of*

*his will, in order that we, who were the first to put
our hope in Christ, might be for the praise of his
glory. And you also were included in Christ when
you heard the message of truth, the gospel of your
salvation. When you believed, you were marked
in him with a seal, the promised Holy Spirit, who
is a deposit guaranteeing our inheritance until the
redemption of those who are God's possession—to
the praise of his glory.* (Ephesians 1:11–14)

What God has promised to do, you can count on it—he
will do. This is the object of our hope. Truly, for those of us
who place our hope in Christ, the best is yet to come.

THE DEFENSE OF HOPE

Many people seem to be naturally hopeful or optimistic.
Yet our hope as a Christian is a very different thing. For us,
hope is rooted in Christ and the gospel. Because our hope is
grounded firmly on the person, promises, and inheritance of
Jesus Christ, it provides us with a defense against the inevitable
setbacks and discouragement that we face in this life. We need
something stronger than simple optimism if we are to endure.
We need hope as our defense against the Deadly Ds that attack
our faith and perseverance. Here is how hope defends us from
disappointment, discouragement, depression, and despair.

DISAPPOINTMENT

The first of the Deadly Ds, disappointment, seems almost
run-of-the-mill. After all, everyone faces disappointment. Yet

this routine experience is potentially deadly to our faith, depending on how we deal with it.

It is natural and normal to become disappointed when things don't turn out quite the way that we expected or the way that we wanted. That is just part of the human experience—the way that God made us. We have goals and expectations, and when something or someone intervenes to keep us from reaching and fulfilling them, we feel let down. That is to be expected.

The problem comes when we let our disappointment take up a prominent place in hearts and stay there. Disappointment becomes unhealthy when we allow it to take the place of gratitude to God. One warning sign that we need to deal with disappointment in a different way is when we begin to feel as though God has let us down. When we start thinking and feeling this way, it is time to face the disappointment head on. We dare not ignore it and hold it inside. It will eventually boil over. Nor should we gripe about our disappointment to every person that crosses our path.

It is best to simply talk about your disappointments with no more than one or two trusted individuals. Some people find all the relief they need in just talking with God about their feelings of disappointment. By doing so, they almost immediately begin feeling more upbeat and hopeful. Others, in addition to talking with God, find it helpful to talk with another trusted individual about the disappointment they are feeling—someone who can listen, empathize, validate, and convey the love of God to them. These glimpses of hope will help you deal with disappointment before it becomes deadly.

DISCOURAGEMENT

The second Deadly D is discouragement. It may come when experiencing not just one disappointment but a series of them. We may begin to suspect that the goals and expectations we have set for ourselves and our ministries are out of our reach, or may not come as quickly as we had hoped. Discouragement hits us at a deeper level than does simple disappointment and is typically harder to shake. As the word implies, it brings a loss of courage that causes our faith to fade.

In Christian life and ministry, discouragement commonly results from comparing what God is doing in our lives and work to what God is doing in others. That makes us feel inadequate, unnoticed, or unblessed. It replaces our confidence in God with self-pity. Here again, the defense is hope. One of clearest examples of this comes from the prophet Elijah, recorded in 1 Kings 19. Elijah had just experienced almost unfathomable, miraculous, public success of the kind that would make a preacher a household name today. Yet, almost immediately, he was overcome by discouragement:

> *Elijah was afraid[and ran for his life. When he came to Beersheba in Judah, he left his servant there, while he himself went a day's journey into the wilderness. He came to a broom bush, sat down under it and prayed that he might die. "I have had enough, Lord," he said. "Take my life; I am no better than my ancestors." Then he lay down under the bush and fell asleep.*
> (1 Kings 19:3–5)

That is a picture of discouragement. Another prime example of discouragement in the Bible is when John the Baptist was imprisoned and began to wonder whether Jesus really was the Messiah. Here is how Matthew described it: "When John, who was in prison, heard about the deeds of the Messiah, he sent his disciples to ask him, 'Are you the one who is to come, or should we expect someone else?'" (Matthew 11:2–3).

Hope was the antidote to discouragement in both instances. For Elijah, God made a special appearance to remind the prophet of His power, then gave him a new mission. Elijah's future orientation was restored, and his discouragement evaporated. To John, Jesus sent back the message that John's own work was reaching its fruition in that of Jesus: the deaf heard, the lame walked, and good news was preached to the poor. That assurance gave John the courage needed to face his own death, which foreshadowed Christ's. Hope is our defense against discouragement.

DEPRESSION

A third Deadly D seems to be increasingly common in our society: depression. The word *depression* is used in various ways, and it is important that we understand which meaning we are using here. Many people understand depression as a feeling of deep sadness. To them, it means being emotionally deflated and not easily encouraged. This type of depression is real and significant. It can affect a person's quality of life and hinder them from being everything God has called them to be. Still, that person is able to manage in life, to take care of their responsibilities, and to hold out hope that things will get better.

This type of depression may arrive for a season and then depart when circumstances improve.

Another type of depression is deeper and darker and may not improve even when circumstances change. This kind of depression often has a medical cause as well as an emotional one. It is best diagnosed and treated by a mental health professional.

While either type of depression may be experienced by those in ministry, we are focusing here on the milder form—the situational sadness that occurs due to our circumstances and how we deal with them emotionally. In this sense, this milder form of depression can be understood as discouragement that decides to settle in and hang on for a time. The best way to deal with this type of depression is to surround yourself with hope. Seek out a trusted friend or counselor who has your true interests at heart. Allow them to point you back to the person, work, and inheritance that is yours in Christ. Spend time with your brothers and sisters in Christ. Worship God. Pray. These actions will rekindle hope within you and lift your sights away from the gloomy present to God's glorious future.

DESPAIR

The fourth and final Deadly D is despair, which is the outcome of unattended depression. Despair occurs when we are at a point where we feel ready to give up hope entirely. This manifests itself in many ways. One fairly common way is ministry burnout. Burnout happens when a person works in ministry—whether professional or volunteer ministry—without the necessary help and support, without adequate rest and nourishment, or without seeing any type of tangible, satisfying results.

Despair can settle around us like a thick, dark cloud, making it difficult to remember that we have a calling. It can cause us to doubt whether God is active and at work within our lives. It can make us question whether God does indeed have a plan and a purpose for our life or whether we have simply been deceived into thinking He is guiding us each step of the way. Unfortunately, many walk away from ministry or fall from their positions of ministry each year due to an overwhelming sense of despair.

Jesus himself verged on despair on the night of His betrayal. He prayed in the Garden of Gethsemane with a full and clear comprehension of everything He would have to experience and endure to accomplish His mission: betrayal by a close friend, abandonment by other close friends, being arrested, falsely accused and convicted, flogged, and ultimately crucified and left to die. Looking ahead at His imminent future, Jesus seemed ready to despair. Yet He overcame that through prayer and was able to restore Himself to a place of hope. Here's how the Gospel of Mark describes it:

> *They went to a place called Gethsemane, and Jesus said to his disciples, "Sit here while I pray." He took Peter, James and John along with him, and he began to be deeply distressed and troubled. "My soul is overwhelmed with sorrow to the point of death," he said to them. "Stay here and keep watch."*
>
> *Going a little farther, he fell to the ground and prayed that if possible the hour might pass*

*from him. "Abba, Father," he said, "everything is
possible for you. Take this cup from me. Yet not
what I will, but what you will."*
(Mark 14:32–36)

In the letter to the Hebrews, we discover Jesus' secret to
maintaining hope. It provides an example for us to follow
when we are tempted to despair:

> *Therefore, since we are surrounded by such a
> great cloud of witnesses, let us throw off everything
> that hinders and the sin that so easily entangles.
> And let us run with perseverance the race marked
> out for us, fixing our eyes on Jesus, the pioneer and
> perfecter of faith. For the joy set before him he en-
> dured the cross, scorning its shame, and sat down
> at the right hand of the throne of God. Consider
> him who endured such opposition from sinners,
> so that you will not grow weary and lose heart.*
> (Hebrews 12:1–3)

Jesus was able to endure for one simple, but profound reason: He believed and knew the best was yet to come. The same
is true for you.

ANOINTING IN ACTION

Hope is the firm belief that the best is yet to be in your life
and in your ministry. This future orientation touches every aspect of your being—mind, emotions, and will. And this is not

mere optimism or wishful thinking. Christian hope is founded firmly on the person, work, and inheritance of Jesus Christ. This hope will give you the ability to withstand the disappointment, discouragement, depression, and even despair that may come to you as you wait for God's anointing on your life and ministry. Here are some actions you can take now to embed hope into your life.

First, examine your life to see where hope is most needed. Is it in your vision of the future (your mind)? Your expectation of God's anointing (your heart and emotions)? Or perhaps in your anticipation (the actions you take based on hope)? Make an action plan to strengthen the area where you need hope the most.

Second, list for yourself the promises of Christ that give you hope. Refer to the Bible, and label each with chapter and verse. Place this list in a place where you can easily refer to it when you feel less hopeful.

Finally, make a contingency plan for when you face one of the four Deadly Ds. The best way to bathe yourself in hope is to surround yourself with hopeful voices. List the faithful brothers or sisters you will rely on when you need hope and encouragement. Be ready to call on them when needed.

CHAPTER 5

Move with God

God never leaves us where we are but always moves us forward. So to receive your anointing, you must be prepared to leave the past behind and move into the future.

Imagine yourself at the age of seventy-five, having had a relatively successful career and a long-term, stable marriage. You are pretty well off and enjoying the rewards of your success. You have a great reputation in the community. People respect you. You're a leader. You are healthy, happy, and mostly content. Just one thing nags you a bit. It's this idea of legacy. You've had an ideal marriage, but you and your spouse are childless. You have built a thriving business, but there is no one to pass it on to. You have had a great life, but somehow you still long for more.

You pray about this, and God answers. He is very specific about what He wants from you—and the blessing He intends

to give you. You want a legacy? You will have it. You long for
a son to carry on your work? You will have tens of thousands.
Your lifelong dream will come true. There is just one require-
ment. You must leave your home, your extended family, everything but your spouse and possessions, and start over. You
will have to move to a distant place where you don't speak the
language or know the customs. No one will know you. You
will be treated as an outsider for the rest of your life. Yes, you
can have God's richest blessing. But to get it, you will have to
move. Will you do it?

Of course I'm talking about Abraham. His story, recorded
in Genesis 12, follows a very similar outline. God offered him
an unimaginable blessing. But to demonstrate his faith in God,
Abraham had to move with God. That is always the case. God's
work is futuristic. It begins in the now, but it leads into the
future. So when we deal with God, we must be prepared to
move with Him.

The same was true for the people of Israel. When God sent
Moses to deliver them from slavery, it meant moving from the
life they knew in Egypt into the unknown of the desert. That
choice was not as easy as you might think. The past, even when
it's negative, can have a powerful effect on us. Compared with
the uncertainty of the future, even a torturous past can begin
to look good. When the Israelites realized they had gone from
being slaves in a land of plenty to being free people in a track-
less wilderness, they got a bit nostalgic. They grumbled against
Moses, saying, "If only we had died by the LORD's hand in
Egypt! There we sat around pots of meat and ate all the food we
wanted, but you have brought us out into this desert to starve

this entire assembly to death" (Exodus 16:3). Every step in the desert brought them closer to God's blessing. Yet they longed to go back.

If you are reading this book, you likely have a strong desire to receive God's anointing in your life and to experience all of the benefits that come with it—in your life, in your church, and for those to whom you minister. That's wonderful! You understand that you are fully qualified for God's anointing. It is His gift to you based on His blood and righteousness. But, like Abraham entering Canaan or the Israelites in the desert, the timetable is unknown to you. You must trust God, ready yourself, and be patient. Above all, it is vital that you keep moving with God. Do not allow yourself to become fearful or discouraged. And, even worse, don't allow yourself to look back to the past. You may long for the past, but it does not long for you. It is done and over with. For better or worse, it will never return, and you cannot return to it. To receive God's anointing, you must be prepared to move with God from disaster to destiny. And you can. To find out how, let's examine the four key elements of that statement.

MOVE

To receive God's anointing, you must move. God's work always involves motion of some kind. That doesn't necessarily mean a change of address, as it did for Abraham and for the Israelites. In some instances, that may be warranted based on what God is calling you to do. And sometimes that change of address is merely a response to your own boredom or impatience. The aspect of movement I have in mind has more

to do with your attitudes and action than with your location. To move with God, you must be willing to change and
grow. That generally comes about when you engage in these
intentional practices.

SHUN IDLENESS

When you feel like God is not moving or doing what you
expected Him to do, it's tempting to become lax and lazy. You
might think, "Well, God seems to be focusing on other things
right now, so I will just take a little break from serving Him."
There are lots of temptations to idleness these days. Many of us
find social media a helpful way to keep in touch with people
that we might otherwise have difficulty staying in contact with.
There are a lot of good things about social media, yet it can be
a tremendous distraction from God's work. If we truly want to
experience God's anointing, we must allow Him to leave a large
footprint in our lives in terms of our time and attention. It is
all too easy to take out your phone or turn on your computer,
thinking you will just check a couple of things, and then spend
the afternoon and evening mindlessly scrolling through frivo-
lous posts. While there is nothing wrong with checking social
media, it's good to keep it in its place, lest we become idle.

Entertainment is another good thing that can become an
invitation to idleness. Streaming services for video program-
ming and music place a never-ending menu of entertainment
options at our fingertips. Again, there may be nothing inher-
ently wrong with the entertainment media we are consuming,
except the quantity of it. When entertainment leads to idle-

ness, it can obstruct us from receiving the blessing and benefits of God's anointing in our lives and ministries.

BE FAITHFUL

The opposite of idleness is faithfulness, and if we want to receive God's anointing, we need to be faithful to His calling on our lives. Moses is a marvelous example of faithfulness. Nearly all of his life revolved around waiting and being faithful rather than actively receiving and experiencing God's blessing. He was chosen by God before birth to deliver God's people from slavery to the Promised Land. During the first forty years of his life, he lived as a prince of Egypt, learning, growing, and waiting for his opportunity to act on his calling. Yet it never seemed to come. When he was forced by his own actions to flee from Egypt, Moses began a second forty-year period of waiting, this time not in a palace but in the desert with a family of wandering nomads.

When Moses was eighty years old, God was finally ready to release His power into his life. This led to a flurry of activity, including the great events we remember Moses for—the ten plagues, the parting of the Red Sea, the receiving of the Ten Commandments at Mount Sinai, and the making of the Tabernacle, the first earthly dwelling place for God's presence.

Then, Moses experienced forty more years of waiting—or wandering, to be more precise—in the wilderness, only to be deprived of actually setting foot in the Promised Land. His entire life, with the exception of a few weak moments, was characterized by faithfulness to God. He was waiting for God to move.

BE PROACTIVE

To be proactive is to take anticipatory action. It means not sitting back and waiting for things to happen to you without forcing God's action for you. To be proactive is to actively do what you know God has called you to do—nothing more, nothing less.

When it comes to releasing your anointing, being proactive means to act in every way as if God is about to bless your ministry beyond your wildest imagination, without demanding that He do so. It means believing that God's Spirit is at work in your heart, transforming you in ways beyond your understanding. It means drawing ever closer to God through Bible study, prayer, worship, and other means of spiritual development and renewal. It means getting off the bench and into the game, serving and meeting the needs of others. It means acting as if the Holy Ghost is on the verge of doing miraculous things in people's lives. But above all, it means trusting God's timing in the midst of all your activity.

GROW WHERE YOU'RE PLANTED

As mentioned before, moving, in this context doesn't usually mean finding another address, location, or ministry position. Instead, it means to be active where you are and to grow where you've been planted. Too often we are more interested in seeking greener grass and calmer pasture than staying put to learn and grow in the ways God wants us to. Too many ministries have stalled or failed entirely because someone didn't have the courage to stick it out when the going got tough.

Rather than wondering what happens in a different setting, real faithfulness involves settling into the ministry and role God has called you to and being "all in" until it becomes crystal clear that God is calling you to go somewhere else or do something different.

The only place you can grow is where you are. The only time you can grow is right now. Rather than constantly looking elsewhere for God's movement, focus on the here and now, where you are. You will certainly recognize many opportunities to grow and be transformed.

WITH GOD

As we move, it is important to move *with God*. That is the only way we can experience all that God has planned for us. Let's think a bit more about Moses and the Israelites, moving toward the Promised Land. This newly formed community had to learn to follow God rather than their own whims, especially after the disastrous time they wanted to move back toward Egypt without God. To make His direction absolutely clear, God provided a simple way for the Israelites to know when to pack up and go and when to stay put. God signaled His movement by providing a pillar of cloud to guide them by day and a pillar of fire by night (Exodus 13:21–22). If the pillar of cloud or fire moved, the Israelites moved. If it didn't, they sat tight. The implication was clear: the people were to move *with God*—and so are we. We don't have so obvious a sign of God's movement to guide us, but there are some ways we can differentiate God's intended direction from our own.

NOT AGAINST GOD

Moving with God means that we avoid moving against God. This takes great spiritual awareness and sensitivity. Yet we do have guidance available to us. We do have instruction. We find it in God's Word. We find it in the still, small voice of the Holy Ghost. We find it in the advice and counsel of a godly mentor or friend. We find it in the community of the saints. When we are sensitive to the various ways God speaks to us and guides us, then we can guard ourselves from moving against God rather than with Him.

One of the most famous examples of a man of God moving against God in the Bible is when Jonah was called to go to Nineveh, proclaim God's message, and invite the Ninevites to repent of their sins. Instead, Jonah booked passage on a ship headed the other direction—a decision that did not turn out well for him. Only after a terrifying encounter with a whale did Jonah turn around and follow God's direction. As a result, many Ninevites repented of their sins and placed their trust in God.

NOT IN SPITE OF GOD

Sometimes, especially for those of us who are anxious to get on with God's plan for our life rather than avoid it, we may be more tempted to move *in spite of* God. In other words, we may seek to do God's will, but in our own way or our own time.

While Moses was known for his faithfulness, there were a few occasions when he was determined to move in spite of God. One was when he saw a Hebrew slave being mistreated by an Egyptian. As the one who had been called to deliver the

Hebrew people, Moses reacted violently, killing the Egyptian and hiding the body. Moses was moving in the right direction, toward the liberation of God's people. But he wasn't moving in God's time and certainly not in God's way. That error caused Moses to spend the next forty years wandering in the wilderness of Midian.

Then, after delivering the people of God from Israel, Moses found himself frustrated by their complaining. When God told Moses to produce water from a rock by speaking to it, Moses chose to strike the rock instead. God still produced the water the wilderness wanderers needed, but it cost Moses dearly. Because of that fit of anger, Moses was not allowed to enter the Promised Land when the years of wandering were over. Beware of imposing your own timetable or plan upon God. Move with Him, not in spite of Him.

NOT AHEAD OF GOD

Another temptation we may face is to move ahead of God. This is the temptation King Saul of Israel faced prior to a major battle against the Philistines. The prophet Samuel had instructed Saul to go to Gilgal and wait there with his troops. Samuel promised to come and offer a burnt offering before the battle, ensuring God's blessing. Here's what happened next:

> *Saul remained at Gilgal, and all the troops with him were quaking with fear. He waited seven days, the time set by Samuel; but Samuel did not come to Gilgal, and Saul's men began to scatter. So he said, "Bring me the burnt offering and the fellowship offerings." And Saul offered up*

the burnt offering. Just as he finished making the offering, Samuel arrived, and Saul went out to greet him.

"What have you done?" asked Samuel.

Saul replied, "When I saw that the men were scattering, and that you did not come at the set time, and that the Philistines were assembling at Mikmash, I thought, 'Now the Philistines will come down against me at Gilgal, and I have not sought the Lord's favor.' So I felt compelled to offer the burnt offering."

"You have done a foolish thing," Samuel said. "You have not kept the command the Lord your God gave you; if you had, he would have established your kingdom over Israel for all time. But now your kingdom will not endure; the Lord has sought out a man after his own heart and appointed him ruler of his people, because you have not kept the Lord's command."

(1 Samuel 13:7–14).

Saul erred in presuming to move ahead of God—to offer the sacrifice himself, rather than waiting for God's prophet, and engage in battle. We may be tempted to do the same when we seek to move ahead of God rather than wait for the Holy Ghost to move and lead us into the work appointed for us to do.

In order to receive and benefit from our anointing we need to move with God—in step with His Spirit. It won't help to get out ahead of God or move in a different direction than God. While you're waiting for God to release His anointing in your life, remain actively engaged with Him and seek to be led by and empowered with the Holy Ghost.

FROM DISASTER

There are two ways to think about moving *from disaster*. First, it is a way to avoid experiencing disaster in the first place. When we move with God's Spirit, following His lead, we avoid many of the pitfalls that can lead to disaster in the life of a Christian. We don't get caught in the snares of the devil when we are moving with and under the protection of God.

Second, moving with God is a way to recover from any disaster you may have experienced. Sometimes, we tend to think that personal failure—whether self-imposed or dictated by the circumstances—disqualifies us from the anointing of God on our lives. We may think that the things we have done in the past prevent us from being of use to God in the future. Nothing could be further from the truth. Remember, God's work is always futuristic. He moves us out of the past and into something new. If anyone can lead us beyond disaster, it's God. He can, and He will. We just have to follow His lead. Here is how that movement unfolds.

FROM HUMILITY

Disaster or failure of any kind does not disqualify us from receiving God's anointing. In fact, it seems almost to be a prerequisite for blessing. Most great leaders seem to have endured some humbling experience that prepared them for a lifetime of fruitful ministry. God has to humble us before He can use us. He has to correct our self-perception before He can pour out his anointing.

For the apostle Thomas, the humbling moment came after his refusal to believe the truth about the resurrection of Jesus. He insisted that all of his intellectual questions be satisfied first. He wouldn't believe until he could put his hands inside Jesus's wounds. For Peter, it was denying that he even knew Jesus, not once but three times. His inflated sense of his own courage had to be pierced. For Paul, humility came after being knocked to the ground from the back of a donkey and blinded by a bright light. His exalted view of his own rightness had to be shown for what it was as he was, literally, knocked to the ground. Even Jesus—who needed no humbling—humbled Himself by allowing Himself to be punished and executed as a common criminal before being raised to new life with resurrection power.

For you and me, this humbling moment is likely to be something quite different, an experience tailored to expose our false sense of our own worthiness. Keep in mind that it's not the experience itself, but the appropriate heart response that prepares us for our anointing.

THROUGH TRUST

In order to be genuinely humbled, we must learn to trust the One who is doing the humbling at a deeper level. Too often we attribute humbling experiences to the devil and other evil forces. But consider that the devil does not want us to be humble. He wants us to be arrogant, full of ourselves, unable to see our own self-destructive faults. God sometimes allows experiences that help us see ourselves for who we are rather than the image we want to portray to the world.

To experience true humility, we must learn to trust God more fully. We must be convinced He has our best interests at heart. We must believe at the very core of our heart that God truly loves us and wants to anoint us. We must come to see that the "disaster" we have experienced will be used by God to transform our lives.

AWAY FROM THE PAST

Humbling experiences can tempt us to believe that we have arrived at the end—the end of our usefulness, the end of our productivity, the end of our ministry. That can be especially true when we recognize our own fault in the disaster. That might be through failure, a pattern of sin, a history of poor leadership, or a relational blunder. Or perhaps we have been the target of others' wrongdoing—hypocritical behavior toward us, open antagonism, gossip, or untruthfulness. Any of these experiences may cause you to believe that you have reached the end, that you are disqualified from God's anointing.

While it is true that sin can impact our relationship with God and hinder our service, God is full of grace and mercy. And when God is involved, disaster never has the last word. The devil doesn't hold the trump card; God does. God is able to redeem any life and any situation and use it for His purpose and glory. The very fact that you are alive means that the past is not the end of your story. God's movement is always away from the past, whether it was glorious or disastrous. Wherever you have been, it is not where God wants you to stay.

TO THE FUTURE

The disaster that you may see as the end of your usefulness is really a gateway into your future. Sometimes, we have to go through disaster in order to experience everything that God intends for us in our life and ministry. Difficult times in life can teach us many lessons. We may need to learn humility. We may need to grow in trust. We might need to change our perspective. We might need to let go of some things that we thought were too important to release to God.

But once we have been through the refiner's fire—once God has walked with us through and called us out of our own personal disaster—watch out! Because He just might be ready to use you in a way that He has never used you before!

TO DESTINY

When we move with God through and beyond our own personal disasters, we are then ready to embrace and move into our destiny in God. A destiny and that cannot be described by mere dreams and wishes, but can be defined by God who positions you to experience a destiny that has His divine signature on it.

What is your destiny? Some aspects of it are individual to you. God has a unique plan for you that revolves around your own background, personality, gifts, and experiences. No one can tell you what your destiny is or what God has in store for you. That is for you to figure out with God's wisdom and guidance. When you discover your destiny, you will know it because you will see God using you in ways you could not have imagined. That does not imply that that you will become well-known or that your ministry will be the envy of others. But it means that God will use you to make a difference in people's lives in ways that you could not have predicted or expected. Though I do not know your specific destiny, I can tell you at least four things about it.

YOU CAN'T CONTROL IT

Your destiny is totally up to God. Listen to what Jesus told Nicodemus in the gospel of John: "The wind blows wherever it pleases. You hear its sound, but you cannot tell where it comes from or where it is going. So it is with everyone born of the Spirit" (John 3: 8). When someone is truly anointed by God and empowered by the Holy Ghost, there is no telling what God will do with that person. When you receive your anointing, you just have to follow the Spirit's leading; you can't make the Spirit do what you want it to do. That is not how it works. You do God's work, in His time, and in His way—and God will bless your life and ministry.

YOU CAN'T RUSH IT

When you begin to see God's anointing on your life, you may want to experience all of it right now. You may want to see everything happen in a moment. You may want to know what the end of the story looks like. But even when you are under the power and influence of Holy Ghost anointing, you can't rush God. God moves in His own time and way. So relax, be faithful, buckle up, and see where the Spirit leads.

YOU CAN'T AVOID IT

You might be disobedient to God, as the Israelites sometimes were. You might be reluctant to follow where He leads, as Jonah was. You might become impatient with His timing, like the apostle Peter. But ultimately, God is going to accomplish in and through you everything He intends to accomplish. God's will cannot be thwarted. He always accomplishes His purposes. He used Abraham, Isaac, Jacob, Moses, Joshua, Samuel, Saul, David, Solomon, and so many others, with all of their faults and failures. He used people like Pharaoh, Nebuchadnezzar, Cyrus, and others, despite their lack of faith in Israel's God. One way or another, God will use you to accomplish His purposes. How much better though, to be a willing and faithful coworker of God in all that He has planned for us.

YOU CAN TRUST IT

You can rely on God totally for your destiny. As the apostle Paul said in his letter to the Thessalonian church: "May God himself, the God of peace, sanctify you through and through. May your whole spirit, soul and body be kept blameless at the coming of our Lord Jesus Christ. The one who calls you is faithful, and he will do it" (1 Thessalonians 5:23-24). Don't become discouraged by the waiting or doubtful because of the timing. Refuse to believe that being humbled leads to being disqualified. When God promises it, you can count on it!

ANOINTING IN ACTION

God's work is always futuristic. It will lead you from wherever you are now into a better tomorrow. The journey may be long. The way may be riddled with obstacles. You can count on being tested a time or two, and humbled well beyond what feels comfortable for you. That's all part of the process. You are qualified for your anointing, and you will receive it so long as you keep moving with God from disaster to destiny. Here are some practical steps you can take now to continue—or kick-start—your movement with God. Consider ways in which God might want you to move this week. What is keeping you from doing what God is asking you to do? What small steps could you take to get started? Decide on a first step, and then take it!

First, list the factors that make it hard for you to step out with God. Is it fear? Guilt? Uncertainty? Shame? When you have identified this limiting factor, surrender it to God.

Next, do a gut check on whether you are following God—or trying to lead. Are you moving with and not against Him, or in spite of Him? Are you being proactive, or controlling? Lay this out before the Lord, and listen for His guidance.

Finally, define your "disaster." What is the thing that keeps you stuck in the past? A failure? A humiliating mistake? A repeated sin? The feeling of being unworthy? Once you have clarity on what is holding you back, ask the Lord to help you move on. Embrace the learning, the healing, the forgiveness, or the growth that God reveals to you. Then step confidently into your destiny.

PART II

Receive Your Anointing

CHAPTER 6

Receive Your Authority

The Promise Anointing

The Promise Anointing foreshadows what God intends to do in your life. It promises the power of the Holy Ghost to transform you so God can work through you to bring hope and redemption to others.

In the early 1960s, the United States was locked in what became known as the Cold War with the Soviet Union. The threat of an actual war was very real as the emerging science of rocketry allowed nuclear weapons to be hurled great distances. The arms race intensified in the spring of 1961 when Soviet cosmonaut Yuri Gagarin became the first human to orbit the earth in space. Tensions were high.

Six weeks after Gagarin's flight, U.S. President John F. Kennedy issued a bold challenge to the American people. In a speech to Congress on May 25, 1961, Kennedy said: "I believe that this nation should commit itself to achieving the goal, before this decade is out, of landing a man on the moon and returning him safely to the Earth." It sounded impossible. NASA, then a fledgling government agency, had only seven astronauts and had managed its first manned space flight less than three weeks earlier. It lasted all of fifteen minutes. There seemed to be no way of accomplishing this audacious goal.

Yet on July 16, 1969, Neil Armstrong emerged from the Apollo 11 lunar module to take the first steps on the moon. The impossible had become possible in just eight years. How was that accomplished? Obviously, the feat required a tremendous level of funding, research, experimentation, and above all, hard work to complete. The inception, however, was Kennedy's bold challenge, together with the confidence that it could be completed. That moment provided the spark to light a flame of passion that produced this grand accomplishment. That is the power of a great challenge.

Imagine how much greater is the power of a *promise* from God? If a mere human leader can release such vast resources with a single speech, how much more power would be unleashed by a direct promise from God Himself? The possibilities contained in God's Word are limitless. And this is the first anointing you can expect to receive from the Lord, the anointing of Promise. It foreshadows and looks ahead to what God intends to do in your life. This anointing offers the promise of the power of the Holy Ghost to transform you so God can work through you to bring hope and redemption to others. Let's see how this anointing operates by examining the life of King David.

DAVID'S PROMISE ANOINTING

David was not the first king over Israel. That distinction belonged to an outwardly impressive man named Saul. Although from the beginning of Israel's existence, God had desired and promised to be their king and ruler, a time came when their hearts turned from trusting wholly in God, and they desired and demanded to have a human king like the nations around them. At the time, God had been guiding the nation through the prophet Samuel. But as Samuel grew old, the people grew restless. They petitioned Samuel to anoint a king for them, like all the other nations had. Samuel knew it was a bad idea, but he prayed about it anyway.

God was even more displeased. He recognized this request as a rejection of Himself as the true leader of the people. He told Samuel He would grant the request, but that he should warn the people of the consequences of having a king: taxation, conscription into military service, the appropriation of land, and forced labor. Samuel told the people they would regret this choice and asked if they really wanted to go through with it. The people clamored all the more for a king. This was perhaps the most disastrous day in Israel's history—the day they decided that it was not enough to have God reigning and ruling over their nation and their lives.

In response, God instructed Samuel to anoint an outwardly impressive man, one who stood head and shoulders above the rest, to be Israel's first king. That man was named Saul. But Saul's loyalty to God was not as strong as his physique. His heart was fickle, and while he sometimes made a show of following God's leadership, he mostly followed his own heart instead. As a result, God determined to remove Saul as king. Through the prophet Samuel, he told Saul, "Because you have rejected the word of the LORD, he has rejected you as king" (1 Sam. 15:23). With that, the stage was set for Samuel to anoint a successor to Saul.

If God had chosen Saul with the intention of teaching Israel a lesson about their desire for a king, He seems to have chosen the successor to show the kind of heart that is required of a godly leader. God sent Samuel to a small town called Bethlehem to anoint the young man who would follow Saul. It was a choice that was a surprise to everyone involved. God directed Samuel to the house of Jesse, who lived in Bethlehem. Jesse was happy to have one of his sons anointed by Samuel. He began with Eliab, the eldest. Eliab, like Saul, was physically impressive. Samuel was convinced he had his man, but God warned him off. He said, "Do not consider his appearance or his height, for I have rejected him. The Lord does not look at the things people look at. People look at the outward appearance, but the Lord looks at the heart" (1 Samuel 16:7). Jesse had several sons, so he presented them to Samuel one by one, seven in all. And one by one, Samuel announced that God had rejected them.

Don't you have any more sons? Samuel asked. Jesse did, just one, the youngest. But he was out in the field tending sheep. His name was David. And when David arrived, Samuel knew immediately that he was the one to anoint. As the youngest son of a sheep herder from an out-of-the-way place like Bethlehem, David was a surprising choice. But God could see what no man, even Samuel, could see. God instructed Samuel to take out his anointing oil and make David the presumptive king of Israel. On that very day, David's life was transformed in a remarkable way. The Spirit of God became a constant presence in his life, bringing a power that David had never known before. By anointing David as king, Samuel announced and released God's promise for David's life, speaking his prophetic future into existence. This is the power of a Promise Anointing.

YOUR PROMISE ANOINTING

From the story of David, we understand that the Promise Anointing is often unexpected. God's promise on your life may surprise you and others. It may take you in a direction that nobody expected. Remember that you do not qualify yourself for God's work. To receive your Promise Anointing, you must be on the alert for the timing, the messengers, the challengers, and the pitfall that surround it.

THE TIMING

In his letter to the Ephesians, the apostle Paul described this first anointing as a seal placed on our hearts when we receive the gift of the Holy Ghost: "When you believed, you were marked in him with a seal, the promised Holy Spirit, who is a deposit guaranteeing our inheritance until the redemption of those who are God's possession—to the praise of his glory" (Ephesians 1:13–14). The Promise Anointing is not something we earn on our own. It's an anointing that is ours by virtue of belonging to Jesus Christ. Because we are His, the Holy Ghost is ours. Even though we may not experience the power or see the results instantaneously, we have the promise of the ongoing work of God's Spirit in our lives.

The apostle Peter alluded to this truth in a slightly different way when he said, "But you are a chosen people, a royal priesthood, a holy nation, God's special possession, that you may declare the praises of him who called you out of darkness into his wonderful light. Once you were not a people, but now you are the people of God; once you had not received mercy, but now you have received mercy" (1 Peter 2:9–10). Peter says that we have been empowered by the Holy Ghost and have become part of a royal priesthood. As priests of God we have been anointed to experience God's presence and power as we receive the promise from His word.

John the Revelator opened the book of Revelation with an observation that goes even further: "Unto him that loved us, and washed us from our sins in his own blood, And hath made us kings and priests unto God and his Father; to him be glory and dominion for ever and ever. Amen" (Revelation 1:5–6).

As John said, we receive an anointing to be kings and priests in His kingdom. This is the promise we receive—a promise that will be fulfilled as we allow the Holy Ghost's power to influence our hearts and direct our steps. If you are a true follower of Jesus Christ, have put your trust in Him and been filled with the glorious gift of the Holy Ghost, then you are anointed! It's as simple as that.

THE MESSENGERS

Do not underestimate the role of Samuel in David's anointing. It is not always easy to deliver God's message, even when you are absolutely sure it comes from God! So, let's give

Samuel credit because he was the first one to recognize David's potential and God's anointing in his life. God will provide a "Samuel" for you too, a messenger to confirm your anointing.

Many of us have had the wonderful experience of having someone speak the truth and promise of God's anointing into our spirit. Take a moment to think back over the people who have spoken God's prophetic word that gave you a promise of greater usefulness and purpose. Maybe someone said, "I can see God at work in your life." Maybe another said, "I sense the Spirit of God is strong in your life. I believe that God has a powerful anointed ministry for you." Perhaps another said, "I would like to invite you to serve alongside me. I believe you can be a big help to me in my ministry."

If you have never had a Samuel, or a Samuel moment in your life, then please let me have the privilege of being that voice! God's Spirit is already at work. He wants to do great things in and through you. How do I know this? I know this because I know what Jesus did for you at the cross of Calvary. I understand the power of His redeeming blood; I know beyond the shadow of doubt, if you learn to submit, become obedient, and tune your ear to hear His voice, then a spiritual impartation will take place. If you will seek Him and follow His voice, God will use you in ways that you could never predict or imagine.

Thank God for the Samuels in your life. They are faithful to speak God's Word to direct your path and give you a promised end. They are not worried that by lifting you up they will somehow become less. They are not jealous of the calling, anointing or results that God has given to your ministry. They do not have any interest in competing with you; their desire is to facilitate your anointing to the glory of God. They are willing and even eager to speak the prophetic word to you because they know everything God uses you to do will rebound to them in spiritual abundance because they obeyed what God told them to do. They are happy to play their God-given role in releasing you into your own destiny.

THE CHALLENGERS

David had Samuel to affirm his anointing. He also had a number of people who opposed his anointing. These opponents did everything they could to discourage David from rising up to claim his anointing. Two of the most prominent were Saul and Shimei.

The Sauls in your life will be those individuals who are much more interested in drawing attention to themselves and building themselves up than they are in anything God might do in you and through you. They are too focused and interested in their own ascendancy to pay any attention to you or be of any service to you. That is what Saul did to David. Saul recognized David's superior gifts, effectiveness, and true love for God, and it made him jealous. He became an enemy to David. Saul kept David close in order to thwart his rise.

The best response to the Sauls in your life is to leave them in the hands of a just God. They have their own plans, projects, preoccupations, and prestige to worry about. You don't need their attention, affection, or approval to do what God has called you to do. If you seek those things from them, they will feel threatened by you and launch into attack mode. It is best to steer clear of them if you can.

Shimei was another opponent of David. Shimei showed up much later in David's life, when he was facing a particularly low moment. David had been driven from his own palace by a revolt led by none other than his son, Absalom. When David was in retreat, Shimei stood by the road and pelted him with stones, shouting, "Get out, get out, you murderer, you scoundrel! The Lord has repaid you for all the blood you shed in the household of Saul, in whose place you have reigned. The Lord has given the kingdom into the hands of your son Absalom. You have come to ruin because you are a murderer!" (2 Samuel 16:7–8).

The Shimeis in your life will be those who stand on the sidelines and criticize everything you do. They will question your motives, undermine your initiatives, disparage your results, and even personally insult you. They can be both discouraging and infuriating, especially when they attack at a low point, as Shimei did to David. It's enough to make you question your anointing.

Again, the best response to the Shimeis is to ignore them. Don't attack or argue, because there is no arguing with fools. Simply do as David did and keep doing the work God has called you to do. God will deal with the Shimeis just as he does the Sauls.

THE PITFALL

Be careful of the major pitfall associated with receiving the Promise Anointing. Satan will attempt to establish a stronghold in your thinking and try to get you to believe that you are not qualified for the anointing that has been promised. Because the promise is yet to be fulfilled, many times the attacks can be discouraging and make you feel as if it will never happen. Then, a negative inner voice is developed and begins to whisper until you succumb to its negativity and fulfill its evil purpose rather than the divine purpose. But the Holy Ghost would say to you, "Let my voice override your negative inner voice and declare that you are qualified."

No matter what others may say, no matter what the circumstances are and no matter what you feel that you lack, if you genuinely believe God's word and leave your ministry entirely in His hands, then you are qualified to receive God's anointing.

Heed the pitfall. Don't let anyone—including yourself—disqualify you from the work the Holy Ghost wants to do in your life. Be submitted, be obedient and be faithful, for if Christ is in you, you will always have the hope of glory and hear the voice today saying, "You are qualified."

ANOINTING IN ACTION

All that is left then is for you to receive your anointing. Trust that God's Spirit is active and at work in your life and ministry. Do what God has gifted and called you to do, and do it faithfully. Trust that God will work through you. Get in the fight and let God glorify himself in and through you. Here are some things you can do now to step into your Promise Anointing.

First, describe the time when you received your Promise Anointing. You could do this in writing, in conversation, through art, or in some other way that is comfortable to you. Anchor yourself in God's promise.

Second, thank the Samuels in your life. Choose at least one person who has affirmed your anointing and call or send a message of thanks this week.

Third, name your adversaries. Simply identifying the Sauls and Shimeis around you is a great defensive strategy. When you see their character and motives clearly, it is much easier to ignore them.

Finally, step over the pitfall of doubt. Identify the primary reason you sometimes feel or believe that you are not qualified to receive your anointing. If this is something that you struggle with on a regular basis, make plans to talk with a pastor or trusted friend about it and ask them to hold you accountable for avoiding this pitfall.

CHAPTER 7

Begin Your Ministry

The Praise Anointing

There is always a gap between your Promise Anointing and its fulfillment. During this period, your willingness to praise and honor God will be a key factor in releasing your next anointing, the Praise Anointing.

Thomas Alva Edison was the most prolific inventor of the Industrial Age, amassing a total of 1,093 U.S. patents. You probably use several of them every day. The quadruplex telegraph, which allowed simultaneous transmission of two-way communication, paving the way for the telephone, was Edison's invention. The microphone in your cell phone owes its origin to Edison. The motion picture camera, still used to create much of the video content you see, came from Edison. He founded General Electric, which makes everything from jet engines to medical imaging devices. And of course, the granddaddy of all Edison's creations, the light bulb, continues to be used in hundreds of millions of homes, offices, and public spaces every day.

What you may not know is that the man who struck gold over 1,000 times as an inventor also suffered some notable setbacks. The electronic vote recorder, cement as a building material for houses, and the electric pen were notable Edison flops. Although Edison had his share of setbacks, he never became discouraged. Even when the trial and error process included mostly errors, he kept a good attitude. Edison's longtime associate, Walter Mallory, described it this way:

I found him at a bench about three feet wide and twelve to fifteen feet long, on which there were hundreds of little test cells that had been made up by his corps of chemists and experimenters. He was seated at this bench testing, figuring, and planning. I then learned that he had thus made over nine thousand experiments in trying to devise this new type of storage battery, but had not produced a single thing that promised to solve the question. In view of this immense amount of thought and labor, my sympathy got the better of my judgment, and I said: "Isn't it a shame that with the tremendous amount of work you have done you haven't been able to get any results?" Edison turned on me like a flash, and with a

smile replied: "Results! Why, man, I have gotten a
lot of results! I know several thousand things that
won't work." [1]

Edison tried more than 6,000 materials before finding one that would reliably produce light when electric current passed through it: carbonized bamboo. Clearly, the ability to keep a positive attitude in the face of setbacks is a key quality for any inventor.

It is also a vital quality for those who would receive God's anointing. Only in this case, it is not mere optimism that makes the difference in our attitude. It is faith. The Praise Anointing comes as we learn to praise God for what He has done and is doing even as we realize that He has more in store for us than we are currently experiencing.

DAVID'S PRAISE ANOINTING

David's first anointing by Samuel did not bring the immediate fulfillment of everything God had in mind for David. Though he had been anointed as king, a significant amount of time passed—and many stressful events occurred—before David ascended to the throne. David's experiences would have tempted most of us to doubt God's promises, turn our backs, and walk away. Yet it was during this time that David learned not only to trust, but also to praise the Lord in the midst of adversity. When David had learned to praise God for His faithfulness in difficult times, he received his second anointing, his Praise Anointing. Let's read the story of this anointing directly

1. Quoteinvestigator.com, *I Have Gotten a Lot of Results!* Accessed November 13, 2020.

from Scripture. Consider how you might have tended to react in each situation where David found himself. Then, compare how David himself—a man after God's own heart—responded. Make this comparison not to shame yourself or cause yourself to feel guilty, but to see where you might have room to grow in faith and hope.

THE CONTEXT

David demonstrated his faith and hope in God in a big way not long after his anointing, when he alone accepted the challenge to face the Philistine giant, Goliath. As a result of defeating Goliath and serving successfully as a commander of troops, David's name became widely known and his popularity soared as people danced and sang, "Saul has slain his thousands, and David his tens of thousands" (1 Samuel 18:7), Before long, David found that he was being opposed by Saul at every turn and needed to flee in order to avoid being attacked and killed by Saul or his men.

Saul pursued David ruthlessly, and on two occasions David had the opportunity to take Saul's life in his own hands. The first occurred when Saul and his men were looking for David in the Desert of En Gedi:

> *After Saul returned from pursuing the Philistines, he was told, "David is in the Desert of En Gedi." So Saul took three thousand able young men from all Israel and set out to look for David and his men near the Crags of the Wild Goats.*
>
> *He came to the sheep pens along the way; a cave was there, and Saul went in to relieve himself.*

David and his men were far back in the cave. The men said, "This is the day the Lord spoke of when he said to you, 'I will give your enemy into your hands for you to deal with as you wish.'" Then David crept up unnoticed and cut off a corner of Saul's robe.

Afterward, David was conscience-stricken for having cut off a corner of his robe. He said to his men, "The Lord forbid that I should do such a thing to my master, the Lord's anointed, or lay my hand on him; for he is the anointed of the Lord." With these words David sharply rebuked his men and did not allow them to attack Saul. And Saul left the cave and went his way.

Then David went out of the cave and called out to Saul, "My lord the king!" When Saul looked behind him, David bowed down and prostrated himself with his face to the ground. He said to Saul, "Why do you listen when men say, 'David is bent on harming you'? This day you have seen with your own eyes how the Lord delivered you into my hands in the cave. Some urged me to kill you, but I spared you; I said, 'I will not lay my hand on my lord, because he is the Lord's anointed.' See, my father, look at this piece of your robe in my hand! I cut off the corner of your robe but did not kill you. See that there is nothing in my hand to indicate that I am guilty of wrongdoing or rebellion. I have not wronged you, but

*you are hunting me down to take my life. May
the Lord judge between you and me. And may
the Lord avenge the wrongs you have done to me,
but my hand will not touch you. As the old saying
goes, 'From evildoers come evil deeds,' so my hand
will not touch you.*

*"Against whom has the king of Israel come out?
Who are you pursuing? A dead dog? A flea? May
the Lord be our judge and decide between us.
May he consider my cause and uphold it; may he
vindicate me by delivering me from your hand."*

*When David finished saying this, Saul asked,
"Is that your voice, David my son?" And he wept
aloud. "You are more righteous than I," he said.
"You have treated me well, but I have treated
you badly. You have just now told me about the
good you did to me; the Lord delivered me into
your hands, but you did not kill me. When a
man finds his enemy, does he let him get away
unharmed? May the Lord reward you well for the
way you treated me today. I know that you will
surely be king and that the kingdom of Israel will
be established in your hands. Now swear to me by
the Lord that you will not kill off my descendants
or wipe out my name from my father's family."*

*So David gave his oath to Saul. Then Saul
returned home, but David and his men went up
to the stronghold.* (1 Sam. 24:1–15).

A second incident occurred when Saul found out that David was hiding out in the Desert of Ziph:

> *So Saul went down to the Desert of Ziph, with his three thousand select Israelite troops, to search there for David. Saul made his camp beside the road on the hill of Hakilah facing Jeshimon, but David stayed in the wilderness. When he saw that Saul had followed him there, he sent out scouts and learned that Saul had definitely arrived.*
>
> *Then David set out and went to the place where Saul had camped. He saw where Saul and Abner son of Ner, the commander of the army, had lain down. Saul was lying inside the camp, with the army encamped around him.*
>
> *David then asked Ahimelek the Hittite and Abishai son of Zeruiah, Joab's brother, "Who will go down into the camp with me to Saul?"*
>
> *"I'll go with you," said Abishai.*
>
> *So David and Abishai went to the army by night, and there was Saul, lying asleep inside the camp with his spear stuck in the ground near his head. Abner and the soldiers were lying around him.*
>
> *Abishai said to David, "Today God has delivered your enemy into your hands. Now let me pin him to the ground with one thrust of the spear; I won't strike him twice."*

But David said to Abishai, "Don't destroy him! Who can lay a hand on the Lord's anointed and be guiltless? As surely as the Lord lives," he said, "the Lord himself will strike him, or his time will come and he will die, or he will go into battle and perish. But the Lord forbid that I should lay a hand on the Lord's anointed. Now get the spear and water jug that are near his head, and let's go."

So David took the spear and water jug near Saul's head, and they left. No one saw or knew about it, nor did anyone wake up. They were all sleeping, because the Lord had put them into a deep sleep.

Then David crossed over to the other side and stood on top of the hill some distance away; there was a wide space between them. He called out to the army and to Abner son of Ner, "Aren't you going to answer me, Abner?"

Abner replied, "Who are you who calls to the king?"

David said, "You're a man, aren't you? And who is like you in Israel? Why didn't you guard your lord the king? Someone came to destroy your lord the king. What you have done is not good. As surely as the Lord lives, you and your men must die, because you did not guard your master, the Lord's anointed. Look around you. Where are the king's spear and water jug that were near his head?"

Saul recognized David's voice and said, "Is that your voice, David my son?"

David replied, "Yes it is, my lord the king." And he added, "Why is my lord pursuing his servant? What have I done, and what wrong am I guilty of? Now let my lord the king listen to his servant's words. If the Lord has incited you against me, then may he accept an offering. If, however, people have done it, may they be cursed before the Lord! They have driven me today from my share in the Lord's inheritance and have said, 'Go, serve other gods.' Now do not let my blood fall to the ground far from the presence of the Lord. The king of Israel has come out to look for a flea—as one hunts a partridge in the mountains."

Then Saul said, "I have sinned. Come back, David my son. Because you considered my life precious today, I will not try to harm you again. Surely I have acted like a fool and have been terribly wrong."

"Here is the king's spear," David answered. "Let one of your young men come over and get it. The Lord rewards everyone for their righteousness and faithfulness. The Lord delivered you into my hands today, but I would not lay a hand on the Lord's anointed. As surely as I valued your life today, so may the Lord value my life and deliver me from all trouble."

Then Saul said to David, "May you be
blessed, David my son; you will do great things
and surely triumph." (1 Samuel 26 2–25).

In both of these instances, David showed the highest character and complete trust in God. Even though he had been
anointed to replace Saul as king, he did not use that as a pretext
for forcing God's hand or taking matters into his own hand.
Instead, he practiced patience and trusted that God would fulfill his promises in his time. David practiced the posture of
praise. Several of David's psalms are believed to have been written during this time, in between his Promise Anointing and his
ascension to the throne. One of the best-known examples is
Psalm 57, which begins with David's raw emotions about being
pursued and concludes with these words of praise:

My heart, O God, is steadfast,
my heart is steadfast;
I will sing and make music.
Awake, my soul!
Awake, harp and lyre!
I will awaken the dawn.
I will praise you, Lord, among the nations;
I will sing of you among the peoples.
For great is your love, reaching to the heavens;
your faithfulness reaches to the skies.
Be exalted, O God, above the heavens;
let your glory be over all the earth.
(Psalm 57:7–11)

Through the hardship and the long period of waiting, David was becoming the kind of person who could praise God and trust him no matter what the external circumstances may be.

THE OCCASION

The occasion of David's Promise Anointing was King Saul's death in battle. Saul, his sons, and their army were battling against the Philistines on Mount Gilboa when the tide turned against them. Saul's three sons were killed, prompting him to turn to his own sword bearer and asking him to kill him. When the sword bearer refused, Saul chose to fall on his own sword, killing himself.

Yet David refused to take joy in Saul's death, even though it meant that he was a step closer to taking the throne as God had promised. After the battle, when one of Saul's men brought news of Saul's death, claiming to have taken Saul's life with his own hand, David responded in a much different way than the man expected:

"Where have you come from?" David asked him.

He answered, "I have escaped from the Israelite camp."

"What happened?" David asked. "Tell me."

"The men fled from the battle," he replied. "Many of them fell and died. And Saul and his son Jonathan are dead."

Then David said to the young man who brought him the report, "How do you know that Saul and his son Jonathan are dead?"

"I happened to be on Mount Gilboa," the young man said, "and there was Saul, leaning on his spear, with the chariots and their drivers in hot pursuit. When he turned around and saw me, he called out to me, and I said, 'What can I do?'

"He asked me, 'Who are you?'

"'An Amalekite,' I answered.

"Then he said to me, 'Stand here by me and kill me! I'm in the throes of death, but I'm still alive.'

"So I stood beside him and killed him, because I knew that after he had fallen he could not survive. And I took the crown that was on his head and the band on his arm and have brought them here to my lord."

Then David and all the men with him took hold of their clothes and tore them. They mourned and wept and fasted till evening for Saul and his son Jonathan, and for the army of the Lord and for the nation of Israel, because they had fallen by the sword.

David said to the young man who brought him the report, "Where are you from?"

"I am the son of a foreigner, an Amalekite," he answered.

David asked him, "Why weren't you afraid to lift your hand to destroy the Lord's anointed?"

Then David called one of his men and said, "Go, strike him down!" So he struck him down, and he died. For David had said to him, "Your blood be on your own head. Your own mouth testified against you when you said, 'I killed the Lord's anointed.'" (2 Samuel 1:3–16)

Far from celebrating Saul's death, which paved the way for David's ascension to the throne, he went into deep mourning. This is because David trusted in God and God's plan. He realized that even though Saul was a deeply flawed king, he had been appointed by God himself. David would do nothing to oppose God's anointed one. He recognized the death of Saul for the tragedy it was, and he would not celebrate it or allow others to do so.

THE ANOINTING

Sometime after mourning Saul's death, David began to pray and ask the Lord what to do next.

In the course of time, David inquired of the Lord. "Shall I go up to one of the towns of Judah?" he asked.

The Lord said, "Go up."

David asked, "Where shall I go?"

"To Hebron," the Lord answered.

So David went up there with his two wives, Ahinoam of Jezreel and Abigail, the widow of Nabal of Carmel. David also took the men who were with him, each with his family, and they settled in Hebron and its towns. Then the men of Judah came to Hebron, and there they anointed David king over the tribe of Judah (2 Samuel 2:1–4).

After many years of faithfulness in the face of adversity and mistreatment by others, it was time for David to receive his second anointing—to become king. But note carefully the result of David's second anointing: he became king over the tribe of Judah. That was only one of the twelve tribes of Israel. God's promise at David's first anointing had been that David would be king over all Israel. But after Saul's death, he only received a partial inheritance.

David had been faithful to God and had learned to praise God in the midst of much opposition and inconvenience, as well as many potentially frightening incidents. When Saul had been killed, though he didn't celebrate, he almost certainly expected to be made king over the entirety of the nation Saul had led. But God was not yet through testing David's faith, hope, and desire to praise God in every situation. He had to learn to praise God when the results were different than he expected. That praise brought on a new level of anointing from God.

YOUR PRAISE ANOINTING

Many of us want to do great things for God in our lives and ministries, and we have received the promise that this fruit will come. But we have not yet learned to praise God in every situation and circumstance. If you are seeking for God to do more in you and through you, it could be that you still have something to learn in the area of praising God. To grow in your ability to praise God, you must recognize and overcome the challenges to your Praise Anointing and learn the practices that lead to it.

CHALLENGES TO RECEIVING
OUR PRAISE ANOINTING

Praising God during a time of adversity is more difficult that it seems, as you probably already know. None of us is born knowing how to genuinely praise God in every circumstance. Honestly, it's difficult to do. The most natural thing to do when life doesn't go our way is to complain and feel sorry for ourselves. So don't feel bad if you struggle with this. Instead, make it an opportunity to grow in maturity and grace so that you can truly praise God even when you might not feel like it. It helps to understand the challenges to praise.

Opposition and Adversity. Like David, sometimes we can experience opposition or other types of adversity in our life and ministry. When this happens, we have the opportunity to trust God to work out His will and plan in and through us. And yet so often it is easier to focus on the problems we are experiencing rather than God, who is capable of doing far more than we could ever ask or imagine. When we focus on our problems more than our protector, we can forget to praise God for His faithfulness.

Disappointment and Discontent. Imagine if David, after being anointed king over Judah, had complained because God had only given him part of what he was promised. Do you think that would have demonstrated genuine faith and hope in God? Do you think it would have demonstrated the maturity of an experienced saint of God? Of course not! Yet it's the very same temptation we face when things are not going as swimmingly as we had hoped—when God has been active and involved in our lives and ministries, but we have not seen the growth or results we had expected to see. We can be like the young child on Christmas day who looks at all the presents received from generous parents and relatives and can only think of all the things they didn't receive.

Envy and Jealousy. When we are caught up in envy and jealousy of our neighbors and colleagues, it is nearly impossible to give God the praise He deserves. It's all too easy to look at those around us and think that we deserve to be doing just as well as they are doing, or experiencing the same kind of results they are experiencing. We may become so envious and jealous of others that we subtly begin to blame God for treating us "unfairly," and we withhold our praise, offering complaints instead.

PRACTICES OF
THE PRAISE ANOINTING

For some of us, the reason we have not yet moved into our anointing is because we have been distracted by the challenges, and caught in the pitfalls of life and ministry. We have not learned to praise God on the difficult days as well as the good days. So let's take a look at how to grow into our anointing by developing a heart of praise through these intentional practices.

Growth in Faith. Learning to praise God begins with having faith in Him. If you don't have genuine faith in God, you can't truly praise Him. Now, it's likely that most people reading this far in the book are people who have some measure of faith in God. For example, you probably trust God for your salvation. But faith in God is about more than what happens to us after we die. It's also about how we live our lives.

When we have mature faith in God, we believe that God is for us, that He has our back, and that, even if things don't seem to be going our way right now, He is still in control and working behind the scenes to accomplish His will and purpose in our life and ministry. Faith in God means that, ultimately, we don't have to worry about anything, because God has it, and He's going to take care of us.

Most of us are not naturally gifted with this kind of faith. We have to learn it. And we learn it by experience. But we only learn it by experience if we pay attention to our experience and interpret our experience with eyes of faith. Then we can look back and see how God has been faithful and that our worry and fear never accomplished anything. As we seek to be more mindful of how God is active in our life and ministry, we grow closer to maturity in faith. And mature faith praises God—not because everything is going right at this moment, but because God is God; He is with us, and He is for us.

Grow in Hope. As noted in chapter 4, Paul named three great Christian virtues in 1 Corinthians 13: faith, hope, and love. We tend to talk a lot about faith and love, but we often ignore the importance of hope. Having hope in God involves looking ahead to the end of the story, even when we are immersed in the most frustrating, confusing, frightening chapters of the story. Again, most of us are not born with this ability to place our hope completely in God and the story He is writing in our lives. But as we mature in Christ, we learn more and more to live each moment with the certainty that God will make all things work together for our good and for His glory. Growing in hope involves learning what God's promises are and paying attention to how God is fulfilling those promises, even when you don't yet have everything God has promised you.

Praise Anyway. Sometimes we encounter situations that shake our faith to the foundation. We don't know what to say or do. We can't see any way over, under, around, or through the obstacle that has been placed in our path. We may even begin to sense the darkness of hopelessness creeping in. In such situations, the Bible is clear what we need to do; praise God anyway. No matter what we face in any given moment, the one constant you can be sure of is that God is worthy of our praise always. The more we put our praise on—the more we learn to praise God in every situation—the more we will be preparing ourselves to receive God's full anointing on our lives.

ANOINTING IN ACTION

When seeking God's anointing, you will certainly face disappointment and setbacks. Like David, you may even experience direct opposition to your calling. You know that God has given you a Promise Anointing, but others may doubt or oppose it. All of that is to be expected. This period is a time of preparation. If David had not endured his wilderness experience and learned to praise God anyway, he would not have continued on the pathway to God's full blessing. It will be the same with you. When you learn to praise God despite the circumstances you endure or the emotions you feel, you place yourself in line for His Praise Anointing. Don't give up! The best is yet to come. As you are learning to praise God, here are some action steps that can help you along.

First, identify any opposition or adversity you are facing. Don't allow this to be a vague feeling in your mind. Be clear about what is making your life difficult. When you name it, you can praise your way through it. The very practice of identifying it will make it seem smaller and less terrifying to you.

Next, identify your personal obstacles to praise. This may take a bit of time and reflection. You need to develop self-awareness on this point. Prayer, journaling, or conversation with a trusted friend may help. Are you jealous or envious of others? Are you feeling self-pity? Are you disappointed with what God has *not* done for you? Name these obstacles aloud to yourself or someone you trust. Then surrender them to God.

Finally, adopt the practice of praise. Don't wait until life is perfect to praise God. Praise Him now. Identify the blessings God has already provided. Praise Him for his Promise Anointing. Praise Him for His goodness and never-failing love. Praise Him for the end of your story, and our story, which has already been written by the death and resurrection of Jesus Christ. Deny the devil a victory in your life by praising God anyway, as David did. Your praise will be the preparation for God's anointing.

CHAPTER 8

Produce Your Impact

The Power Anointing

The Power Anointing brings God's full blessing to exercise His authority in your life and ministry. But with that power comes responsibility. You will be accountable to use that power in the ways God directs.

"With great power comes great responsibility." Most of us have heard some version of that little proverb. It is sometimes called the Peter Parker principle because it was etched into popular imagination by the comic book hero Spiderman, back in 1962. The idea, of course, dates back much further. A legend from the ancient Greeks makes the point well.

According to the story, Damocles was a member of the royal court of Dionysius II of Syracuse. Damocles was enamored by the power and authority held by the king so he constantly flattered Dionysius, hoping for some elevation in his own status. Dionysius finally offered the younger man a sort of job swap. He allowed Damocles to trade places with him for one day so he could see firsthand what it meant to hold such power. Of course Damocles agreed.

There was a catch, however. Damocles did indeed sit on the throne. But the king had arranged for a sword to be suspended overhead, pointing straight down, held by a single strand of hair from a horse's tail. The sword was a reminder that great power always comes with great responsibility. One misstep, one poor decision, could bring disaster on both king and kingdom. Damocles quickly realized that holding a position of power was not all pomp and privilege and begged to be released from the king's service.

Jesus said, "From everyone who has been given much, much will be demanded; and from the one who has been entrusted with much, much more will be asked" (Luke 12:48). There is a lesson here for all who seek God's anointing. That anointing will be accompanied by power. And those who receive the anointing will be accountable to use that power responsibly. The third type of anointing is the Power Anointing. But this power from God is not, as some suppose, given for our own benefit. The Power Anointing releases a certain share of God's power to us so that we may use it in the way He directs. In other words, the release of power from God brings a great responsibility to God. Let's see how the Power Anointing operated in the life of David, and how you can expect it to function in your life.

DAVID'S POWER ANOINTING

David's Praise Anointing brought him only a part of what the Promise Anointing had foretold. There was more to come. And that further anointing, the Power Anointing, brought David into his full power and authority through the presence and activity of the Holy Ghost in his life. He then had the authority to rule over all God's people, to extend the kingdom, and to increase its influence in the world.

THE CONTEXT

When David received his anointing as king of Judah, he understood that he had received only a fraction of what had been promised. And the Praise Anointing did not put an end to the adversity and opposition David faced. If anything, it intensified. While three of Saul's sons also died in the battle on Mount Gilboa, one son, Ish-Bosheth, survived. Abner, who had been the commander of Saul's army, declared Ish-Bosheth king over all the tribes of Israel except for Judah. This precipitated a war between the house of Saul, led by King Ish-Bosheth and his commander, Abner, and the house of King David, whose army was commanded by Joab.

After a fierce battle at Gibeon, the forces of Saul were defeated, and Abner fled from the battle. Joab caught up with him at the hill of Ammai, where some of the men of Benjamin had rallied to protect Abner. As evening approached, Abner managed to convince Joab to call a truce. But that was not the end of the conflict. In 2 Samuel it says that "the war between the house of Saul and the house of David lasted a long time. David grew stronger and stronger, while the house of Saul grew weaker and weaker" (2 Samuel 3:1). Meanwhile, six sons were born to David in Hebron by six different women. Still, David had not yet received his full inheritance. He was ruler over but a small portion of Israel.

In the end, a feud within the house of Saul brought about its demise. Commander Abner's influence was growing, and King Ish-Bosheth became jealous of him. He picked a fight with Abner, accusing him of sleeping with one of King Saul's concubines. Abner became so incensed that, after many years of faithful service to the house of Saul, he suddenly switched allegiance to King David of Judah.

Abner contacted King David and offered his assistance in bringing the rest of the tribes under David's rule and authority. David agreed on the condition that Abner bring with him Saul's daughter, Michal, who had been promised to David as his wife. Saul had then changed his mind and given her to another man. After securing Michal away from her husband, Abner gathered the elders of Israel:

> Abner conferred with the elders of Israel and said, "For some time you have wanted to make David your king. Now do it! For the Lord promised David, 'By my servant David I will rescue my people Israel from the hand of the Philistines and from the hand of all their enemies.'"
>
> Abner also spoke to the Benjamites in person. Then he went to Hebron to tell David everything that Israel and the whole tribe of Benjamin wanted to do. When Abner, who had twenty men with him, came to David at Hebron, David prepared

a feast for him and his men. Then Abner said to David, "Let me go at once and assemble all Israel for my lord the king, so that they may make a covenant with you, and that you may rule over all that your heart desires." So David sent Abner away, and he went in peace.
(2 Samuel 3:17–21)

But things did not go well for Abner from that point. When David's commander, Joab, and his men returned from a raid and heard that Abner had switched sides, they were furious. Abner had killed Joab's brother in his escape from the battle of Gibeon, and Joab had not forgotten. Joab set a trap for Abner and murdered him. David responded, not by celebrating and rewarding his commander Joab, but by mourning and honoring his fallen foe. This endeared him to the people of the eleven tribes Abner had been trying to deliver for him (2 Samuel 3:28–37).

THE ANOINTING

Even after all that, one thing still stood between David and his full inheritance. Ish-Bosheth was still recognized as king over Israel. And just as he had done with King Saul, David refused to raise his hand against Ish-Bosheth or to try to manipulate events to bring himself to power. He was content to trust in God's timing. However, two of Saul's men were not so patient. Rekab and Baanah could see the way events were trending, and thinking they would get on David's good side, they snuck into King Ish-Bosheth's house at midday and stabbed him to death.

Cutting off his head, they brought it to King David, expecting him to be grateful and reward them richly. David's response to them was much different than anticipated:

> David answered Rekab and his brother Baa-nah, the sons of Rimmon the Beerothite, "As surely as the Lord lives, who has delivered me out of every trouble, when someone told me, 'Saul is dead,' and thought he was bringing good news, I seized him and put him to death in Ziklag. That was the reward I gave him for his news! How much more—when wicked men have killed an innocent man in his own house and on his own bed—should I not now demand his blood from your hand and rid the earth of you!"
>
> So David gave an order to his men, and they killed them. They cut off their hands and feet and hung the bodies by the pool in Hebron. But they took the head of Ish-Bosheth and buried it in Abner's tomb at Hebron. (2 Samuel 4:9–12)

Once again, David chose to honor the Lord's anointed rather than those who sought to take matters into their own hands. Even so, the events of that day greatly clarified the situation for the people Israel. For David, it removed the last remaining obstacle to ascension to power:

> All the tribes of Israel came to David at Hebron and said, "We are your own flesh and blood. In the past, while Saul was king over us,

*you were the one who led Israel on their military
campaigns. And the Lord said to you, 'You will
shepherd my people of Israel, and you will become
their ruler.'"*

*When all the elders of Israel had come to King
David at Hebron, the king made a covenant with
them at Hebron before the Lord, and they anointed David king over Israel.*
(2 Samuel 5:1–3)

After fifteen years or more of adversity and waiting, David had finally come into his kingdom. He had received his
full inheritance. He was in a position to be and do everything
God had in mind when he called him to be king. This was his
Power Anointing.

THE INCREASE

David's Power Anointing did indeed bring a far greater
measure of authority and fruitfulness in David's life and work.
Yet that power was not for his benefit alone. While the words of
Isaiah 9:2–7 are a prophesy about one of David's descendants
rather than David himself, they help us understand the significance of this moment in history:

*The people that walked in darkness have seen
a great light: they that dwell in the land of the
shadow of death, upon them hath the light shined.*

*Thou hast multiplied the nation, and not in-
creased the joy: they joy before thee according to*

the joy in harvest, and as men rejoice when they divide the spoil.

For thou hast broken the yoke of his burden, and the staff of his shoulder, the rod of his oppressor, as in the day of Midian.

For every battle of the warrior is with confused noise, and garments rolled in blood; but this shall be with burning and fuel of fire.

For unto us a child is born, unto us a son is given: and the government shall be upon his shoulder: and his name shall be called Wonderful, Counsellor, The mighty God, The everlasting Father, The Prince of Peace.

Of the increase of his government and peace there shall be no end, upon the throne of David, and upon his kingdom, to order it, and to establish it with judgment and with justice from henceforth even forever. The zeal of the Lord of hosts will perform this.

David wore the crown. He had the power. And yet it was up to David, with God's help, to ensure that his power was used in a manner that was pleasing to God. By his words and actions, he had the capability of bringing greatness to God's kingdom, not just for David's lifetime alone but for generations to come—and even to us, through Christ. Just as in the words of the prophecy, the battle was over, and there was an opportunity for *increase.*

In David's time, under his reign, this increase would involve a variety of different aspects. Under David's leadership, there would be opportunities to increase the borders of God's kingdom, the land of Israel, as various local tribes were conquered and driven out and power consolidated under David's throne. There was the possibility of increased security as David amassed a powerful army to protect his people from enemies and invaders. There was the opportunity to increase the nation's wealth, as the people were largely freed from the burden of self-protection to seek prosperity. And there was the opportunity to increase their influence in the world as the nation grew great and became a regional and world power. Ultimately, this increase would bring forth the Messiah, the savior of all nations. All of this was within David's reach as the ruler over God's united kingdom.

THE LOT AND THE LINES

David's success and the nation's increase were not a foregone conclusion. Much would depend on how David exercised his authority and used his influence. The prerequisite for the increase is found in the very same prophecy in Isaiah 9: "The government shall be upon his shoulder." Now, that's not a fancy way of saying that David is in charge and everything depends on him. Far from it! What it means is that while David was making decisions, he needed to let God call the shots. Even though the people looked to him as king, he needed to look to God as the ultimate ruler. If he allowed God to govern him, he could be assured of success and increase; but if he refused God's government over his own life and the kingdom, there would be trouble. In order to experience the increase, he needed to submit to government, that is, to God's authority.

David's situation was identical in this way to the people of Israel who followed Joshua into the Promised Land. One of the miracles and great blessings of the Promised Land was that everyone was going to be a property owner. Each family would have its own cut, its own portion, its own share, its own lot in the Promised Land that would be their inheritance, that would stay in their family, and that they would pass down from generation to generation. But in order for each family to receive their inheritance, the land had to be surveyed and subdivided. Lots had to be clearly defined. Lines had to be drawn, so everyone would know what belonged to whom. The book of Joshua lists these lot lines in great detail (see Joshua 15:1–12). This gives us the principle of the lots and lines. Each person was given property, a certain "lot." But that property was limited by the "lines" of boundary. So it was with King David. He had received his lot—his promised inheritance—when he was made King over all Israel. But in order to prosper in that role, he needed to stay within the lines of that lot. He had to remember that while he was king of Israel, God was ruler over all. In other words, with great power comes great responsibility. We are accountable to God for the power with which He entrusts us.

YOUR POWER ANOINTING

As with David, so too with you. If you are faithful, there will come a time when you have the opportunity to step into your full anointing—to receive everything God has for us in this life. I am not talking here about financial wealth or other material things, although some people may certainly be blessed in that way. I mean the spiritual wealth that comes from maturity in Christ and faithfulness to His calling. To step into this anointing, you must understand the four key aspects of the Power Anointing in your life: the lot, increase, government, and lines.

YOUR LOT

Your lot is the unique set of circumstances and opportunities that God has placed before you. Each of us have been given a lot by God. Our lot is unique to us as individuals. Nobody else's lot is exactly like yours, and your lot will never be exactly like someone else's. Some aspects of your lot were specifically chosen for you by God. Other aspects of it have more to do with the experiences you have had in life.

One aspect of your lot is your personal background. You did not choose anything about your birth, including the date. Your lot would have been much different had you been born four thousand years before Christ. That would have had a major impact on who you are and what types of things you were able to accomplish in life. Your lot also includes where you were born. It makes a difference whether you were born in the United States of America, China, or Australia. Also, nobody asked you what family you wanted to be born into. Frankly, some people have tremendous advantages because of their family background while others have less favorable experiences growing up. Yet all of these things were specifically chosen by God to shape your life and your service to Him.

Another aspect of your lot are the things that have happened to you in life—whether you experienced them as positive and affirming or negative and destructive. Some of us live privileged lives, while others face more hardship. Some people enter adulthood feeling loved and valued and having a strong sense of purpose, because key people poured themselves into their lives; others lacked meaningful connections and entered adulthood feeling lost and alone. Some were abused or otherwise traumatized. All of these things contribute to our "lot in life."

The good news is that no matter what your lot is, God can and will give you the opportunity to serve meaningfully in His kingdom. No matter where we start in life, God desires to give us the satisfaction of a life filled with purpose.

YOUR INCREASE

Your increase is the potential you have for personal and kingdom growth. I cannot tell you what kind of increase you can expect to see when God releases your anointing. That is as individual as one's lot—and perhaps even more so. What I can tell you is that God wants to release the full power of the Holy Ghost through your anointing into your life and ministry. And when that happens, nothing can stand in your way. No power—visible or invisible—can stand against you when the Holy Spirit guides your steps. He will give you the increase. And even if it's different than what you originally desired, it will be more meaningful and better than you can possibly imagine. When you receive God's increase in your life, it will benefit not only you, but many others; and the benefit is not only for today but for generation after generation.

I strongly encourage you not to think of your increase in terms of material wealth. God can certainly give that in abundance if He so chooses. But God is not bound to give you wealth any more than He was required to give you life. God can do whatever He pleases. If He chooses to bless you with abundance, it will not be for your enjoyment alone. God's increase is always given for the benefit of others.

The increase you can count on is the increase of God's image in you. He wants to make you more and more like Him. He will help you grow in godliness, drawing you into deeper and deeper levels of holiness. You might think, "Well, that doesn't sound all that exciting. Give me something I can hang my hat on. Let me see something that will increase my status in the world." If that is your motivation, you are not seeking the kingdom of God. You're looking to serve yourself and God does not honor that. God doesn't bless self-promotion. Instead, like David, we need to trust that God knows what He is doing and trust that He has our best interests at heart. And rather than grasping for things that are not ours, believe that God's plan for your life will be far more eternally interesting and exciting than anything you could plan on your own.

YOUR GOVERNMENT

Your government is the rule of God in your life. God's increase is never given without His government. God's favor does not rest on those who seek to be self-directed. God's blessing does not fall on those who are trying to do things their own way. If we want to experience God's increase in our life and ministry, we have to be willing to receive His government over every aspect of our lives. Yes, even over those aspects of our lives that seem hidden from other people, God sees and He knows. God wants you to submit to Him in every area of your life.

One of the reasons we don't see an increase in our lives and ministries is that we don't want any increase in God's government over us. We think there is already enough as it is. We must be open to greater authority in our lives if we want to see a greater release of God's power.

Receiving God's government is a matter of trust. So many of us are most familiar with a government that we cannot fully trust. Throughout time, most individuals have had to guard against government that would take advantage of those under its power, plunder their best resources, and enrich those at the top without a thought for the people below. For many of us, it is a radical thought to believe that we can so fully trust someone that we give them complete authority over us. Yet that is God's invitation and expectation for us. He wants us to believe that He is on our side, that He has our back, that He has a glorious plan for our life, and that if we give Him full power over lives, He will bring never-ending increase. That's what faith looks like. It is our willingness to receive God's government, trusting in His goodness and benevolence.

YOUR LINES

Your lines are the boundaries of your authority in the use of God's power. To see an increase in power, you must prove yourself faithful at staying within those lines. You may think, "I cannot handle another line in my life! Everybody is drawing lines around me. I don't want to stay within the lines I've already got." But you need boundaries. We all do. You need someone other than yourself to tell you what is right and wrong. You need someone to hold your conscience accountable. It doesn't matter who you are, what you have accomplished, or how God is already using you. You need boundaries in your life. And the lines are not just for laypeople. Preachers need them too. If we are going to receive our inheritance, we've got to accept the lines God gives us. You can probably think of examples of prominent leaders who have stepped outside their lines. The results are always tragic. We must accept God's authority in our lives if we are going to have authority over others. With the Power Anointing, you will step into a release of God's power that can break every yoke. To use that power effectively, you must remain within the bounds that God sets for you.

Personally, I'm glad when God steps into my life and tells me to get back in line. When He corrects my attitude or checks some behavior that tends to go in the wrong direction, I rejoice. I hope you can do the same. Let the Holy Spirit keep you in check. And remember that He may do that through the voice of a faithful counselor or friend. When you allow God to point you in the right direction, there is no limit to how far you can go.

ANOINTING IN ACTION

The Power Anointing brings God's full blessing to exercise His authority in your life and ministry. But with that power comes responsibility. Your anointing will release a certain share of God's power, which is your lot. It is to be exercised under His authority, or government, not your own. And you will be accountable to use that power in the ways God directs. You must stay within those lines. When you are faithful in these ways, you can expect to see an increase both in your own holiness and in the impact that you have on others. Your life will be transformed in ways you cannot yet imagine, and you will see that transformation multiplied in the world around you in the name of Christ. You will receive power when the Holy Ghost comes upon you.

Here are some practical steps you can take now to prepare for your Power Anointing. First, describe your lot. What are the unique abilities and advantages God has given you? What are the difficulties of the circumstances within which He has placed you? Understand yourself and your lot, and praise God for it. Remember the connection between your praise and the release of God's power.

Second, pledge yourself again to live and labor under the government of God. If there are areas of your life in which you have resisted God's authority, confess and surrender them now. You will never be given more power than you can responsibly handle.

Next, seek God through prayer on the matter of your lines, or the boundaries of your work. Where does God want you to be active? What are the limits of the work He is giving you? Ask the Spirit for clear guidance on where, when, and how you should act on His behalf.

Finally, pray for an increase. Ask the Holy Ghost to bless you with power so you can be fully transformed into Christ's likeness and see an impact through your work.

CHAPTER 9

Reclaim Your Joy

The Personal Anointing

The Personal Anointing is one that we give ourselves during times of discouragement or adversity as a reminder of our anointing by God. When we do, God honors our boldness and faith in seeking Him and grants the power to overcome.

The life of King David reads like a hero's tale. He seems larger than life, like a man able to leap tall buildings in a single bound. David's exploits were indeed grand. He was a great leader and a godly man. Yet he was a man, and he had the usual frailties of human nature. One of the lowest moments in David's life came when he was on the run from King Saul, who was trying to kill him. To escape, David and his men took the unusual step of taking refuge in the land of the Philistines, arch enemies of Israel. Achich, king of Gath, gave David the town of Ziklag to use as a base for his men and their families. David was not playing the traitor. He remained loyal to Saul, despite Saul's attempts to kill him. But David needed a place of refuge, and he found that among the Philistines, where he would be out of Saul's reach.

Sometime later, David and his men returned from the battlefield to find that their town had been burned to the ground and their wives and families captured by the Amalekites, yet another warring people in the region. David was devastated. He and his men wept aloud until they were exhausted. They were exiled from their country, on the run from their own king, and prey to enemies all around them. They had lost everything. This was the first real challenge of his leadership. The men were angry and bitter, having lost their families. There was even talk of mutiny. Some of David's own men wanted to kill him. As a man and as a leader, David had come to the lowest point of his life.

We know that this was not the end of David's story. He would go on to take the throne and extend Israel's borders far beyond the territory of Saul. But to finish the story, we have to connect the dots. How did he get from here: alone, exhausted, and under threat even from his own men, to there—enthroned, exalted, and remembered as Israel's greatest king? We find our answer in 1 Samuel 30:6. There we read the words that form the great pivot in David's fight. These words mark the bottom of his descent into opposition and discouragement and the beginning of his rise to victory: "David encouraged himself in the Lord his God."

While Bible scholars have typically identified three anointings in David's life, the three that we have already discussed, my study has revealed to me a fourth anointing, a Personal Anointing. We typically think of an anointing as an act in which one person anoints another. But in this particularly intense situation in David's life, he took the extraordinary step of "anointing" himself, and God honored his decision to do so. The Personal Anointing occurs when you seek the release of God's blessing to overcome a hardship or personal failure. In these moments, God may honor your boldness and faith in seeking Him and grant you the power to overcome.

Let's examine a second experience of Personal Anointing in David's life. Through this example, you will understand what the Personal Anointing is and how it can operate in your life.

DAVID'S PERSONAL ANOINTING

A second time disaster struck David was in the aftermath of his sin with Bathsheba. Let's begin by taking a closer look at the circumstances that led to this instance of Personal Anointing and the impact it had on David's life and leadership.

THE CONTEXT

After David became king over all Israel, he began driving rival nations and people from the land, uniting the twelve tribes, and establishing a central government and place of worship. Among other things, David conquered Jerusalem and made it his capital city, then brought the Ark of the Covenant to reside there. David wanted to build a temple to house the Ark. It would be a dwelling place for God among His people. It seemed like a good idea, even to the prophet Nathan, who affirmed David's plan. But the Lord came to Nathan later that same night and contradicted Nathan's advice. God said:

> *Go and tell my servant David, "This is what*
> *the Lord says: Are you the one to build me a house*
> *to dwell in? I have not dwelt in a house from the*
> *day I brought the Israelites up out of Egypt to this*
> *day. I have been moving from place to place with*
> *a tent as my dwelling. Wherever I have moved*
> *with all the Israelites, did I ever say to any of*
> *their rulers whom I commanded to shepherd my*
> *people Israel, 'Why have you not built me a house*
> *of cedar?'"* (2 Samuel 7:5–7)

God went on to say that it would not be David but one of his offspring who would build a temple. David would enjoy a time of rest from his enemies, and his throne would be established forever. But the honor of building the temple would not belong to David, but to the next generation. David did indeed see success in his endeavors, establishing the kingdom of Israel more securely than Saul was ever able to do. But success brought another kind of problem to David, distraction from his purpose that led him to take advantage of his position and seduce a woman named Bathsheba:

> *In the spring, at the time when kings go off*
> *to war, David sent Joab out with the king's men*
> *and the whole Israelite army. They destroyed the*
> *Ammonites and besieged Rabbah. But David re-*
> *mained in Jerusalem.*

One evening David got up from his bed and walked around on the roof of the palace. From the roof he saw a woman bathing. The woman was very beautiful, and David sent someone to find out about her. The man said, "She is Bathsheba, the daughter of Eliam and the wife of Uriah the Hittite." Then David sent messengers to get her. She came to him, and he slept with her. (Now she was purifying herself from her monthly uncleanness.) Then she went back home. The woman conceived and sent word to David, saying, "I am pregnant."
(2 Sam. 11:1–5)

David's distraction led to temptation, which led to an abuse of his power and ultimately, disastrous consequences. Upon learning that Bathsheba had become pregnant, David then set about to cover up what he had done. He brought Bathsheba's husband, Uriah, home from the battlefield, in hopes that he and others would assume the baby was Uriah's. But Uriah refused to sleep with his wife while his fellow soldiers were at battle. Eventually, David concocted a plan to put Uriah in an extremely vulnerable position in battle, a plan that led directly to Uriah's death. After allowing Bathsheba a short time of mourning for her husband, David brought her to the palace to be his wife and to raise the child as his son.

However, David's scheme did not go uncontested. God revealed to the prophet Nathan what David had done. Nathan confronted David with a story about a wealthy man who had coveted his neighbor's sheep, eventually murdering the man to gain possession of it. David was outraged. He said, "As surely as the Lord lives, the man who did this must die! He must pay for that lamb four times over, because he did such a thing and had no pity." Then Nathan said to David, "You are the man!" (2 Samuel 11:5–7). Nathan further revealed that while David's life would be spared by God, the child conceived through his illicit union with Bathsheba would die. When the child became ill, David pleaded with God to spare the boy's life. He fasted and spent the nights lying in sackcloth on the ground, refusing food. This went on for seven days, until the child finally passed away. This disaster was in some ways worse than the raid on Ziklag because it was brought on by David himself. Rather than being tormented by external enemies, David was at odds with God.

THE ANOINTING

After the boy died, David's attendants were reluctant to break the news to him for fear of his reaction. But David noticed them whispering amongst themselves and forced the question. "Is the child dead?" he asked. "Yes," they said simply. "He is dead" (2 Samuel 12:13–19).

David's sin had led to disaster—a disaster that could have easily derailed his destiny. What would he do next? Rage at the servants for delivering bad news? Fall into despair? Rail at God for His judgment? Scripture tells us what David did:

> *Then David arose from the earth, and*
> *washed, and anointed himself, and changed his*
> *apparel, and came into the house of the Lord, and*

worshipped: then he came to his own house; and
when he required, they set bread before him, and
he did eat. (2 Samuel 12:20)

At the lowest point of his life, when anyone might have forgiven him for letting his grief consume him, David did the unexpected. He anointed himself. To be sure, this was a different type of anointing than the three described earlier in the book. It was not a ceremonial anointing demonstrating other people's recognition of his power and authority. But the fact that the same word was used is likely not a coincidence. Where David had been anointed three times before by others, this time—in the midst of personal disaster—he anointed himself.

Those around David were confused. They had seen him under great personal distress. They knew how much the baby's life meant to him. They were so shocked that they asked David about it. David's response was clear-eyed, full of faith in God and fully understanding the responsibility that was upon his shoulders. He said, "While the child was still alive, I fasted and wept. I thought, 'Who knows? The Lord may be gracious to me and let the child live.' But now that he is dead, why should I go on fasting? Can I bring him back again? I will go to him, but he will not return to me" (2 Samuel 12:22).

It would be a mistake to take this incident in David's life as a prescription for all grieving parents. David's situation was unique in many ways. Not all who grieve the loss of a child should be expected to respond in the same way. The lesson here is one for leaders. At a time when David could have reacted by feeling sorry for himself or lashing out at others, he chose to look ahead. He understood that he could not do anything about the past but he could do something about the future. He had a job to do in leading God's people, and he anointed himself yet again for that job.

THE SIGNIFICANCE

In one sense, this Personal Anointing pales in significance to the other three. This was no official act by the elders, religious leaders, or political operatives of any official government or institution. It was a private, personal act conducted in David's own home. Yet the act held tremendous significance in his life and leadership.

First, it was an acknowledgment of his disaster. David had been hoping that the child would survive. While David was still hopeful, he remained entirely focused on the child. He fasted, he put on sackcloth, and he refused to do anything other than attend the baby. The fact that he arose from that place, got cleaned up, anointed himself, and began to eat was not an indication that David wasn't grieving; instead, it was an acknowledgment of the reality of David's disaster, the child's death.

Second, it was an acceptance of his ongoing responsibility. While David's child was ill, he literally put everything else in his life on hold. That not only included personal matters but professional matters as well. While he was focused on the child, David did nothing to maintain or advance the kingdom of Israel. He was simply unable to focus. Getting up from the child's bedside was an indication of his acceptance of other responsibilities that would not allow him to continue to sit on the sidelines.

Third, it was an indicator of his need for renewal. David's anointing of himself was a physical act that acknowledged this fact. He had been anointed in the past, but he felt the need for a fresh anointing. He needed to be renewed and refreshed for the task at hand.

Fourth, it was conducted with the knowledge that no one else was going to do this for him. If it was going to be done, he had to do it himself. David's disaster was such that no human being could help him or bring an end to his pain. No pep talk or encouraging words can help a grieving parent refocus on what else needs to be done. That motivation had to come from within. David's self-anointing was an acknowledgment of his need to persist and be faithful to God's calling on his life.

By anointing himself, David acknowledged the reality of his situation and owned his share of the blame. He also closed the door on the past, reaccepting God's call on his life to lead well in the future. This self-anointing placed David back in position to exercise God's power, under God's authority, for the furtherance of God's will.

YOUR PERSONAL ANOINTING

There may come a time when you need to anoint yourself for God's service. David's example sets an important precedent. His anointing was not assuming or usurping something that didn't belong to him. It was a re-affirmation of what God had already promised and released in his life. In the same way, our Personal Anointing does not precede or supersede God's anointing on our life. It confirms God's anointing and makes it real in our life.

If you are qualified for your anointing by faith in Christ, and if others have recognized and confirmed your anointing, there is nothing to prevent you from giving and receiving Personal Anointing when you need it. Again, Personal Anointing is not an attempt to manipulate God or force Him to so something that He is unwilling to do or has not already done. It as an act of faith that simply recognizes and affirms God's grace and anointing in your life. To effectively use this blessing, you must understand the four keys to Personal Anointing.

THE NEED FOR PERSONAL ANOINTING

The first key to using the Personal Anointing is to understand when it is needed. There are three primary occasions for this anointing. Let's examine each one.

Personal Disaster. When you experience personal disaster in your life, like David did, you may have to pick yourself up, remind yourself of God's call on your life, and keep putting one step in front of another. You can't always count on having an encourager close by. Sometimes you have to encourage yourself.

Yet this does not mean that you have the power to absolve yourself of sin. If your disaster involves private sin, you must confess it to God and repent of it. It's no good anointing yourself again for God's service if you feel no remorse for, or intend to continue in the same old sin. Personal Anointing is incompatible with obstinance in sin. Also, if your sin has injured another person, confess to that person if possible and make restitution. If you need help with conquering that sin—and you probably do—consider confessing to someone you trust and asking him or her to hold you accountable. Then and only then can you proceed with Personal Anointing.

If that disaster involves a public fall, the situation is even more complicated. If you have sinned publicly, it's important that you confess and repent publicly and seek to make amends for any harm that was done. Submit to the authorities over you, and follow any prescribed remedies, rehabilitation, or restoration plans. When you are released again for ministry, then you may benefit from a Personal Anointing.

Personal Discouragement. Another circumstance that may call for Personal Anointing is when you are feeling intense personal discouragement in your life and ministry. Sometimes life throws us a curveball. Ministry can be tough. We can find ourselves wondering why things are not turning out the way that we expect or why we aren't getting the results we hoped for. We may even begin to question the gifts God has given us, the calling He has placed on our lives, or the anointing He has released for our ministry. In such a case, you may need the reassurance of Personal Anointing.

Adversarial Opposition. Adversity in our lives and ministries is another situation that calls for reaffirmation of our anointing. Whether it is based on jealousy, a difference of philosophy, or personal reasons we don't understand, you may encounter those who oppose your ministry. Some people seem to have no ministry of their own but take joy in sniping at others in hopes of preventing their success. In such cases, it is important to remind ourselves of our gifts, our calling, and anointing. Personal Anointing is a powerful way to do that.

THE BENEFIT OF PERSONAL ANOINTING

The second key for using the Personal Anointing is to understand its benefits. We have already hinted at some of the reasons why personal anointing may be beneficial. Let's make those benefits more specific.

Affirmation. Sometimes we need someone to tell us that we are doing something right and that God is at work in and through us. In certain situations, the best person to do this—the only person truly capable of doing this—may be ourselves. So we can anoint ourselves to affirm our faith in God and His faith in us.

Courage. If the challenges and opposition we face in life and ministry are causing us to be dispirited, we need to receive courage. The source of our courage must always be the knowledge that God has gifted us, called us, and released His anointing in our lives. If we need a little bit more courage to face the dragons and giants that stand in our way, we need look no further than God's presence and anointing. Personal Anointing is a great way to find the courage we need to continue through adversity.

Strength. We are aware of our personal weakness. On some days, we don't know how much more we have to give. We must remember that the source of our power and strength is not from within. Our source is the God who created the entire universe, breathed life into us, and gave us a job to do. If we are searching for strength, there is only one reliable place to turn.

By reaffirming God's anointing in our live, we recognize and release God's power and strength in our life.

Determination. Whether we are talking about life or ministry, it is better viewed as a marathon than a sprint. While there are times we struggle to get through the day, the only way we are going to finish the race is to find an inexhaustible source of determination. That is why the author of Hebrews directed us to look to Jesus, the author and finisher of our faith (Hebrews 12:2). Personal Anointing reminds us that our own sense of purpose and determination comes not from ourselves but from the Christ who saved us and gave us a plan, the promise, and the power to overcome.

THE HOW OF PERSONAL ANOINTING

The third key to using the Personal Anointing is understanding how to actually do it. If you hope to come out of your disaster and step into your destiny, you will have to learn how to anoint yourself. You must learn to take everything that God has ever spoken to you at a church meeting, every prophetic word you have ever received from a Samuel, and pour it back into yourself. There will come a time when you will doubt all these things, and perhaps even doubt the existence of God. When that happens, recall every prophetic work spoken to you and every blessing you have ever experienced and repeat it to yourself. You may need to get out your journal and reread the passages that speak about your anointing or how God has delivered you. When there is no kind voice to be heard anywhere, go to your prayer room and anoint yourself with oil. In these critical moments, the words you speak to yourself can bring either defeat or victory, death or life. Speak the promises of God and His presence into your life. Anoint yourself to continue the battle.

THE PITFALL OF
PERSONAL ANOINTING

The fourth key to using the Personal Anointing is to understand the pitfall associated with it. You may be wondering if anointing yourself allows the possibility of claiming self-glory or self-aggrandizement. Yes, that possibility exists. The temptation here is to substitute your own power and glory for God's. That is, to believe that you are empowering yourself through this anointing rather than placing yourself in touch with God and His calling on your life. That danger is very real.

The remedy for this pitfall is found in Amos 6:6: "They drink wine in bowls and anoint themselves with the chief ointments, but they are not grieved for the afflictions of Joseph." In other words, for the Personal Anointing to be effective, your motivation must come from a heart that is breaking for those that are hurting around you. As long as you want to use your anointing to help deliver somebody else who is grieved by affliction, it is safe to anoint yourself. When your motivation is to build yourself up for your own sake rather than for others, you should not attempt Personal Anointing.

ANOINTING IN ACTION

The Personal Anointing is an anointing you give yourself to remind you of God's anointing on your life and place yourself in touch with His power. It is like the woman who suffered from constant bleeding, recorded in Mark 5. No one was willing to help her. No one was praying for her. No one was trying to bring her to Jesus. Yet she thought, "If I just touch his clothes, I will be healed." And she was. When you face adversity or discouragement, there may be no other person who can encourage you. When you learn to encourage yourself in the Lord through the Personal Anointing, you will keep moving from disaster to destiny. Here are some practical steps to experiencing the Personal Anointing.

First, consider the circumstance or people that cause you to question your anointing or to lose heart. Is there anyone who can speak a prophetic blessing into your life to encourage you? If not, this may be a moment when you need to reconnect with God's power through a Personal Anointing.

Next, prepare for your personal anointing. If you do not have anointing oil, obtain some. Find a quiet place where you can commune with God, perhaps in the presence of your spouse. Recall the promises God has given you through Scripture and through the prophetic confirmation of other believers. Review them. Thank God for them.

Then, check your heart. Are you simply feeling self-pity or wishing for more attention or thanks for your labors? Or are you genuinely questioning the anointing of God in your life? Are you doing this just so you can feel better? Or are you seeking to be empowered to continue the work you are doing for others? If you detect a selfish motivation, speak with the Lord about it. Ask Him to adjust your attitude.

When your heart is clear, anoint yourself with oil and speak God's Word to yourself. Remind yourself of your salvation, your anointing by the Holy Spirit, and the call to service He placed on your life. Remind yourself that you are fully qualified by faith and that your ministry is vital to those around you. Rest in God's presence and blessing.

Finally, get up and get back to work. The purpose of your Personal Anointing is to recharge you for effective ministry. Rest and refresh yourself as needed, then continue the work God has called you to do.

Step into Your Anointing

If there is one thing that I want you to take away from this book, it is that you are qualified for your anointing, and nobody can take that away from you. As long as you live, there will be someone who tries to disqualify you from God's anointing. They may continually remind you of your past and the sins that have been covered by the blood of Jesus. Or they may watch you closely, hoping to catch you in some misstep or failing. They may criticize you for some aspect of your life or the way in which you serve others.

When that happens, remember the woman caught in adultery (see John 8). She was apprehended in the very act of disqualifying herself. She was surrounded by accusers, and her situation looked bleak. Her very life was in danger. But when her accusers brought her to Jesus for judgment, they completely misjudged the situation. You see, they had brought the *dis-*

qualified to the *qualifier*. He refused to condemn the woman but sent her back with a charge to live a transformed life, one that would be a blessing to both her and others.

When others try to throw you around, let them throw you at the feet of Jesus. He will stoop down in the dirt with you. He will place His strong hands upon you and say, "I requalify you for salvation, for holiness, for ministry. Rise and go!"

You are fully qualified to receive God's anointing to empower your own transformation and the transformation of the world around you. Do not doubt this. And in the name of Jesus, I say to you: Receive your anointing. Claim your inheritance. Rise and go forth to serve in His name.